A Cappella Pop

A Complete Guide to Contemporary A Cappella Singing

By Brody McDonald

Foreword by Deke Sharon

Published by
Alfred Music Publishing Company, Inc.
PO Box 10003
Van Nuys CA 91410

alfred.com

ISBN-10: 0-7390-8627-8
ISBN-13: 978-0-7390-8627-8

"Chapter 24 Making A Recording" excerpts from *On-Time and On-Budget* by Freddie Feldman
Used by kind permission of VOCOMOTION
© 2009, 2012 FREDDIE FELDMAN
Published by VOCOMOTION
All Rights Reserved
www.vocomotion.com

Project Editor – Michael Spresser
Associate Editor – Anna Wentlent
Layout/Design – Matt Koprowski

This book is dedicated to my wife, Marty McDonald, whose love and support I could not live without; my parents, Don and Dessie McDonald, who supported all my dreams and raised me right; my college choir director, RD Mathey, who shaped me into the teacher I am; and my extended family at Kettering Fairmont High School— where students, parents, colleagues, and alumni have helped the vocal music program grow into something special beyond measure.

Table of Contents

Foreword
by Deke Sharon

There is no accredited pathway to studying contemporary a cappella. At least, not as of the time this book is being published.

Contemporary a cappella was born and nurtured on college campuses and by young professional a cappella groups looking to find a way to effectively replicate the sound of popular music, which is increasingly driven by strong beats and dense instrumental textures. This process is nothing new, as several vocal idioms in our nation's history—barbershop, doo-wop, vocal jazz—developed in clubs, barbershops, and on street corners, before gaining a measure of legitimacy.

People began to teach these new musical forms, although they themselves had not been formally educated in a scholastic environment. How does one translate knowledge and experience into a successful, methodical pedagogy?

And what if you don't have the benefit of learning by doing, but rather already teach in a school, and want to bring this new sound and style to your students? Cue video montage of a high school music teacher learning by trial, error, and instinct, as they frantically juggle an unstructured mix of concerts, CDs, rehearsals, workshops, web sites, and discussions.

Brody McDonald's path to contemporary a cappella followed this rocky route. He called me one day, intoxicated by the possibilities of having his students sing the music they listened to on their own, but with absolutely no other knowledge of contemporary a cappella. With no formal programs available, I steered him in the direction of a handful of resources and wished him luck.

Brody is both methodical and indefatigable, and before long he was not only directing an award-winning high school group, but found himself a resource for other directors.

You might find it interesting that the aspect of Brody's directorship that impresses me the most is not his musicality. There are many skilled music directors who, year after year, bring out the best in their singers. This is deeply admirable, but not unique. Rather, the element he possesses, which most directors do not, is his understanding of and commitment to the entire musician, performer, and person. In addition to being musical mentors, directors often find themselves in the position of life coach, personal counselor, and psychiatrist. But I had never before heard of an individual director teaching his singers personal comportment and interviewing skills in addition to vocal production and mic technique. It reminded me of the old Motown hit factory, where Diana Ross et al were taught not only how to sing, but how to be stars, one haircut and choreographed routine at a time. Music is communication, and communicating via music is about much more than the notes.

Brody brilliantly shepherded his ensemble, Eleventh Hour, to be the first high school a cappella group in a televised national vocal competition. More impressive is the fact that he teaches at a public school, and draws choir members at random from his district (not a magnet performing arts academy or the like). Even more impressive is the fact that his group sang arrangements with each voice on a separate part. With no ability to hide behind another stronger singer, there were no weak links. These young singers had more in common with Take 6 than a high school choir. I think of them as a once-in-a-decade vocal ensemble . . . but I might revise my estimate if I haven't heard another like them ten years from now.

But all of this is beside the point now. That's history. What interests me is you.

Yes you, the person reading this book.

You're obviously interested in learning how to create a successful ensemble and don't want to reinvent the wheel. Excellent.

Take Brody's sage advice to heart . . . and know that it's just the first step.

Where do you go from here? If I knew, I'd tell you.

How about this: you go figure it out, create the next amazing a cappella ensemble, and maybe one day you and Brody will end up creating the first formal educational program specifically about contemporary a cappella.

I'll be there, on the first day of classes, sitting in the front row.

—Deke Sharon

Deke Sharon is the founder of The Contemporary A Cappella Society, a co-founder of BOCA, the ICCA tournament, and a successful professional a cappella group, The House Jacks.

Introduction

There is no limit to what a man can do or where he can go, if he doesn't mind who gets the credit.

—Father Strickland
19ᵗʰ Century Jesuit

If you are reading this book, you're interested in a cappella and looking to learn more. I was (and am) exactly like you. By the time you read this, I will have finished my eleventh year with an a cappella group in my high school choir program. Their name is Eleventh Hour, and as it says on the cover, they were the first high school group to ever be selected for NBC's a cappella reality TV show *The Sing-Off.* You might guess that I've been doing a cappella forever, and that I was involved in a collegiate group while I was earning my music education degree. That couldn't be further from the truth. I'm about to tell you the story of how a very unlikely person came to embrace an art form that would change his entire musical career. I don't know if you will find it interesting. If you start to get bored, skip past this introduction and get on with the rest of the book! But I write this story because it illustrates that you can start at *ground zero* and become a successful a cappella director. You'll have a better chance than I did, because you have more help than I had and because a cappella is much, much bigger than it used to be.

When I was in college at Bowling Green State University, I wanted nothing more than to eventually be a college choir director. That might still happen; who can say? I was heavily involved with the choral program at BGSU, singing in the Men's Chorus, Collegiate Chorale, as well as operas each year and many lab ensembles for conducting students. I was also bitten by the barbershop bug.

At the time, Richard D. Mathey was the director of choral activities at BGSU. RD (as he insisted on being called) was a longtime barbershopper. He not only programmed barbershop arrangements for the Men's Chorus and Women's Chorus, but he also auditioned students for the "Varsity Quartet," a barbershop quartet that sang several selections on the Men's Chorus concerts. I tried for years before finally making it into the Varsity Quartet. Unfortunately, we weren't very good. Still, I broke into the "inner circle" of barbershop fanatics at Bowling Green. Hanging out with the other, more experienced, barbershoppers really opened up my musical world. I never actually planned to be a music major, you see. It was by dumb luck that I got on that path. My musical tastes were about as broad as any major album-oriented rock radio station. I owned every album by Led Zeppelin, The Who, The Doors, Pink Floyd and Frank Zappa, and had little idea what else existed in terms of music.

Soon, I was listening to a lot of barbershop. I was enthralled. My friends had pretty extensive CD collections, and soon musical tangents from the barbershop realm exposed me to groups like The Real Group, Voices of Liberty (from Disney's EPCOT Center), Glad, and Take 6. I liked them well enough to explore a cappella a bit further. My first CD purchase was the soundtrack to Spike Lee's PBS special "Do It A Cappella." I figured that I'd get to hear several groups on one CD, like a sampler. I just about wore that CD out, and was more interested in a cappella in general. Still, it seemed like there wasn't much out there to get my hands on. That wasn't true, but in those days the internet hadn't fully come into being. I wanted more exposure to a cappella, but I didn't know where to go to get it.

One year, when I was at the Barbershop Harmony Society's annual convention, I was given a free a cappella sampler CD called *Voices Only*. It had tracks from The Blenders, The Bobs, The Coats and many other groups of whom I'd never heard. I had heard of Rockapella, and their track on the sampler was "Bed of Nails," which I really dug. Still, a cappella was a novelty to me.

Soon I got my first high school teaching position, where I still teach today: Kettering Fairmont High School (in a suburb of Dayton, Ohio). When I took the job, I inherited a show choir. I had zero exposure to show choir, and didn't know what I was doing. Still, I was determined to learn and to do a good job. The program was in okay shape, but most of the talented students I had were in the show choir. If I was going to build something worthwhile, I had to keep those kids happy while I did it.

Show choir competitions meant Saturdays full of long bus rides, long hours, and long waits. In order to build rapport with the kids, I started teaching them barbershop tags to sing in the cafeteria after our performances were over. I also started passing my CD collection around the bus (this was before iPods, you see), in hopes that my kids would begin to like something besides show choir. *There is nothing wrong with show choir*, but these kids knew nothing but. That's a sad situation, no matter what the genre.

One of my show choir boys was also a drummer in the marching band. After hearing "Bed of Nails," he decided to put together a group to perform it for our Spring Variety Show. He couldn't come up with the sheet music, but after some searching did find the song "Johnny" as performed by the 17th Avenue All-Stars (on the same sampler). He got a group of five guys to sing it, and it was a huge hit.

About the same time that spring, I toyed with the idea of forming an octet to sing community engagements. Many organizations (Rotary Club, Lion's Club, etc.) were calling to request the show choir, but ended up not having enough space to host us. I wanted to sing light choral music like Disney's Voices of Liberty. At the audition for eight spots, I had only eleven singers. They were all about equal in ability, so I took them all. One of the kids said her Mom suggested we be called Eleventh Hour because eleven kids got in at the last minute, and it stuck.

In our first year, we bounced around a bit, singing light choral music as I had planned. We got a cold call from Tiffin University's Up In the Air (www.upintheair.us). They were looking for a school to fill a hole in their fall tour. I accepted and they arrived. I had no idea what they were going to do, but honestly I wasn't turning down a free show. They sang a cappella and world music. They did the whole bit—vocal percussion and instrument replication (even including a didgeridoo on one song). We were hooked. THIS is what we wanted to become.

I started trying to chase down any a cappella sheet music I could find, but there wasn't much. We were singing stock arrangements of "The Lion Sleeps Tonight" and "Stand By Me." It was okay. Then I stumbled onto www.casa.org. At the time, they were offering free arrangements from their library with membership (a practice that has since been discontinued). I waded through hand-written jumbles of songs, trying to find some good pop tunes. That helped for a while. We were rehearsing only an hour a week after school, but making some decent sounds.

Soon, Eleventh Hour was growing in popularity. They got to do a lot of gigs in town because they were portable in a way the show choir wasn't. After a few years, there were so many auditionees that Eleventh Hour wound up being all seniors. I knew I was going to have a problem on my hands if I had to start from scratch each year that way, so I started a "junior-varsity" group called Fusion. I didn't have much time to give them, so they kind of had to fend for themselves. This was a real turning point for us. The kids in Fusion were having so much fun working on their own that soon they were challenging Eleventh Hour as fan favorites.

The first year I had Fusion kids move up into Eleventh Hour was a breakthrough. They were singing so well, we were asked to open for LeAnn Rimes at a local arena. With that gig booked, we decided to also try our first foray into competition. The National Championship of High School A cappella (NCHSA) is now defunct, but we gave it a run. It didn't work for us, being eight singers in a scenario where we had to use zone microphones, but it did motivate us to increase our practice schedule (and the experience of singing for 3,000 LeAnn Rimes fans will have such an effect). We also called Deke Sharon (who seemed to have a grasp on this a cappella thing, having founded CASA and also having published some arrangement books) and commissioned our first custom arrangement.

By the end of that season, the parents of those kids were adamant that we record a CD. Each family kicked in and we were soon in the studio. Well, we were in someone's basement for two days, singing between bunches of quilts hung to make "booths," but you get the picture.

After the first CD, we started building momentum. Soon we were recording each year, and receiving some awards. There is an association called the Contemporary A cappella Recording Awards (CARA) that opened a high school division. It's like the Grammy® Awards for a cappella. Our second CD won Best High School Album and Best High School Song. You probably know by now that high school kids like awards.

I had taken my chamber choir to the Ohio Music Educators Association conference a few times, so I decided to take a chance and submit Eleventh Hour. We were selected to perform and also to present a session for teachers about how to get started with a cappella groups. We prepared for these events by scheduling a multi-day tour of the state. Eventually, we ended up at OMEA several times, ACDA Central Division in 2010, and even ACDA National in 2011. In the whole span of Eleventh Hour, I think that ACDA National is tied for our proudest moment. The other moment . . . well, that's a story unto itself.

The biggest single growth experience for us occurred in the fall of 2009, when we were contacted about a new television show called *The Sing-Off*. Producers had seen videos of us on tour and wanted us to come audition. After checking the website and telling the casting company there must be some mistake (it said ages 18 and up), I was told they weren't going to take "no" for an answer. Since my daughter had just been born, I was unable to go. A valiant parent booster stepped in and took the kids to Chicago.

Unfortunately, the kids failed their audition. They told me it seemed like everyone wanted them to do well, but they froze under the pressure. I wasn't surprised. This was in the fall, and the group had only been practicing about a month. Still, every member said the same thing: "I wish we would've given more energy." That became a rallying point for the rest of the season. Any time I saw effort lagging or stale performances I said, "Do it again, and do it like you wish you would've done it in Chicago."

In the spring of 2010, it was as if fate was smiling on us. *The Sing-Off* had done well in the ratings, and NBC was casting a second season. Once again I heard from the casting producers, whose job it was to find as many talented groups as possible for the selection process. I pulled the kids into my office and we had a very serious talk. I told them that if they really wanted a second chance, there could be nothing less than full commitment.

The audition was going to be in Chicago again, even in the same location. I had the students tell me everything about that first audition. Everything. What was the building like? Where did they hold the groups waiting to audition? Where did they go first? How big was the audition room? Who was in the audition? Since there was an interview component, what was that room like? What questions did they ask? What questions *might they ask?* We made a complete map of the audition from start to finish, and started practicing. We didn't just practice the music. We practiced every last detail. We planned how to enter the room, who was the default spokesperson, who would answer specific question topics, how to "dish off" or "save" an interview question that was floundering, etc. We knew that every group on the show had to have some form of identity, so we even worked on ensuring the casting company would know what ours was.

The rest is, as they say, history. We made the second season and it was a life-changing experience. Don't get me wrong; being on national television is not a requirement for having a good group. Quite the contrary—I think there are many amazing groups who didn't make it. Still, the lesson of *The Sing-Off* was the same lesson as every one we've ever studied: *practice makes permanent, perfect practice makes perfect.*

Let's be honest, *the unknown is scary*. The reason we succeeded in getting on *The Sing-Off* is that we took our mistakes from the Season 1 audition and turned them into plans for success in Season 2. Perhaps you purchased this book because you have some unknowns you want to turn into knowns. That's great. It's really the only way to make things work. While I was forced to learn a cappella in the school of hard knocks, there's no reason you have to. Whenever I can save myself time and headaches, I do. My hope is that you can use this handbook to do just that.

As you read, you'll notice several guest contributors. They are wonderful, amazing, talented people. I have learned a lot from them and from many others. Over the past decade, I have learned from so many wonderful "aca-people" that I can't possibly list them all. Again I will say—*you don't have to go it alone.* Without the combined efforts of students, colleagues, parents, and a cappella mentors, I would never have grown so much over ten years. I encourage you to reach out and build a community for yourself to foster the growth of your group. Good luck with your journey. If there's anything else you ever need, just give me a call. We're all in this together.

—Brody McDonald

How to Use This Handbook

Thanks for purchasing and/or reading this handbook. Well, it's really more of a *guidebook*. I call it that because there's no substitute for the fearless experimentation I hope you do. This book is here to make sure you have the knowledge you need to make educated decisions as you experiment rather than flail around blindly. It is to keep you from reinventing the wheel, so to speak.

The chapters aren't in a hard-and-fast order, although I tried to keep some semblance of flow from the beginning stages of development through more advanced topics. Still, each chapter stands on its own and serves as a reference for its specific topic.

For example, if you don't have a group yet, you'll likely want to start by reading **The Audition**. If you have a group in place, you could skip that chapter and come back to it before your next round of casting. Maybe you are in the middle of your season and what is on your mind *right now* is how to make sense of microphones and other sound equipment. You could just jump to **Live Sound for Pop A Cappella.**

There is no *right answer* for any of the thousand questions you'll encounter on your road to excellence in contemporary a cappella. There are only many options, some of which will work for your program (and many that won't). I think you'll find that many of the ideas and practices contained in these pages will work, because I only included things that have worked for me over the past decade. I also sought out advice from the best a cappella professionals to give you the best knowledge from specialists in their fields.

Because this book contains contributions from many wonderful collaborators, I attempted to unify the tone by staying in the first person throughout. However, please know that the "first person" is sometimes someone other than me . . . and sometimes is a blending of multiple people. Those who pitched in on this project are selfless, wonderful musicians. I hope you will support them, because they are fellow evangelists for the art form of a cappella. There are many groups, arrangers, vendors, and such in the wide world of contemporary a cappella, but I believe those whose knowledge is contained here to be guaranteed winners.

A friend of mine once said, "Being a musician is like walking to Montana. You better like walking." That has proven to be true. There's no guarantee you'll ever get to Montana, and even if you do, it won't happen quickly. Still, there is joy in the walking. Like any other exercise, the more you walk, the stronger you'll get. We're all equally distant from perfect, and we're all walking to Montana. Thanks for joining us, and enjoy your walk.

Getting Started

CHAPTER 1

WHAT ARE WE, ANYWAY?

> ❝*Begin with the end in mind.*❞
> —Stephen Covey

Welcome to our guidebook. I say guidebook rather than handbook because there is no one way to run your a cappella group. Not only is there more than one way to skin this proverbial cat, there's more than one type of cat.

What defines an a cappella group? Isn't barbershop "a cappella?" Can't vocal jazz be sung "a cappella?" Hey, wait a minute . . . our chamber choir sings madrigals "a cappella." Throughout this guidebook, we'll use the word "a cappella" to mean *contemporary a cappella,* also sometimes known as *pop a cappella.* This means that the group is recreating popular music by imitating the sounds of a band. Guitars, horn lines, bass guitar, and even the drumset are there to support the soloists. This concept of a "vocal band" is one that we will explore and embrace.

At first blush, contemporary a cappella might come across as fluff—the dessert after dinner. After all, any group that sings rock, pop, hip-hop, or funk is really just a gimmick, right? This isn't "real music." This is just the bait to lure students in, so we can teach them all about classical music. It's the old "bait-and-switch" where *Glee*-esque pandering opens young singers' minds, allowing us a chance at getting them to sing Brahms, Mozart, Poulenc, Whitacre, and the like. Not so. I'm here to say that just isn't the case. Contemporary a cappella has great educational value. It has real merit. It requires skill. Chops.

Public awareness of a cappella is on the rise. Between Rockapella's commercials for Folger's coffee, group numbers on *Glee,* and the appearance of NBC's *The Sing-Off,* a cappella has been seen by tens of millions of Americans. At one time, a cappella might have had an image problem. It has often been parodied and lampooned (think

Andy Bernard on *The Office*), but even that parody has lead to acceptance. Can you think of another American musical form that at one time was considered a novelty? How about jazz? Once upon a time, jazz was an indulgence, a playground for late-night musicians steeped in cool rather than technique. Over time, jazz was studied and found to have real merit. It became academically institutionalized and is now respected as an **art form**. We're here to say that a cappella is also an art form.

Why can't we use music from the Top 40 as a teaching tool in our choirs? We can and we should. If you're a teacher, you know that first we have to know where the kids **are**. After that, we can figure out what direction they should move to improve, as well as what might motivate them. Pop music is familiar. It's fun. That helps.

Once we've connected with kids, what do we do? The answer goes far beyond "get them to eat their veggies by promising dessert." Sure, we use fun music or membership in a select after-school group as a motivator. On top of that we must illustrate to students why a cappella can help them. Let's look at the educational benefits of a cappella. A cappella develops an individual's skills in many areas:

» *Collaboration*: Working together as an ensemble.

» *Improvisation*: "Riffing" solos or adding harmonies to an arrangement *just because it sounds cool.*

» *Evaluation*: Singers must constantly listen to each other and adjust to improve their overall sound.

» *Emulation*: Singers must know what sounds they are trying to make (guitar, drum, horn, backing vocals, solo, etc.) and figure out how to emulate them.

» *Independence*: Singers will have to sing in small sections, even down to just one on a part.

» *Tuning*: With only voices in the mix, there's nowhere to hide. Singers must learn to sing in tune with each other.

» *Keeping time*: Singers must keep time to ensure all sections of the group stay together.

» *Visual presentation*: It's just you and that microphone. The world is watching, so look alive.

Let's face it—a cappella is the new chamber music. It's fun, interactive, and frankly . . . **challenging**. It's a dream come true for us choir directors. Now that I've convinced you it's worth doing (and given you some ammunition against those who think you're "selling out"), let's figure out what type of group you should have.

When I took my first high school job, I inherited someone else's program. That means I started off by working in someone else's format. I had to find what worked for me, or actually, for *us*. A cappella became a great fit for us. The reason I believe that a cappella is for everyone is because it is the most flexible genre around. The variety of music available to you is endless, from 60's soul to present day Top 40. You can have a cappella groups of virtually any size, talent level, or combination of gender. Only have a few boys in your program? How about creating a select men's group to make singing look more cool to guys in your school? Do you have a show choir that just isn't your strong suit? Turn them into a large a cappella group with lighter choreography. Is your program currently very small? Just six good singers on microphones can impress your whole community.

If you haven't started a group yet, you'll want to decide which configuration fits you, then jump over to the chapter on **Auditions**, as everything else in this book deals with an existing group.

So how do you decide what type of group to have?

The first rule is that there are no rules. Most a cappella groups range from 4-16 singers on individual microphones to as high as 17-32 singers without amplification. Ensembles can be male, female, or mixed. You can do whatever you want, but follow this simple guiding principle as you start: **begin with the end in mind**. Think about your program. Think of your best, brightest, most reliable, and musically talented kids. How many are there? Do you have a mixture of boys and girls, or a majority of one sex? Do you have a need to include a lot of kids, or is this group going to augment an already purposeful program? Do you want to get into individual microphones or go with either zone or no microphones?

By answering those questions, my hope is that you have begun to settle in on what type of group you want. For instance: "I can see it now . . . 16 of my best kids—eight guys, eight girls." Or, "Better to start with just a few upperclassmen I can trust." Or, "We have good sound equipment, so I could just do six men on mics. That can help us recruit more guys." Or even, "My show choir is 24 kids right now, so we could do a few a cappella tunes and see how it goes over." Don't forget to play to your strengths as a teacher. If you work best with small groups, emulate Sonos, Rockapella, or Take 6. If you gravitate towards more kids, replicate Voices of Lee, On the Rocks or Straight No Chaser.

Once the membership of the group is set, you must have an idea of your identity. Remember your Shakespeare: "To thine own self be true." Truer words were never spoken, but how many organizations truly know themselves? In order to be successful as an a cappella group, I believe you need to take three big steps:

1. Define your group

2. Know your audience

3. Craft your image

Define Your Group

The first step sounds like the easiest, but in many ways it can be the toughest. We struggled with it for years. I wanted an octet singing light choral music, like Disney's Voices of Liberty. My students had other thoughts and other strengths. Over time, we have evolved into a "one-on-a-mic"/vocal-band style group, like Rockapella or Take 6. In the beginning, our numbers ranged as high as 11, but we eventually settled into

Eleventh Hour, a group with seven singers. We also formed a 16-voice mixed feeder group called Fusion in response to increased audition demand over time.

What do you want to be? Don't feel constrained by where you are now. Will this be a male, female, or mixed group? The answer shouldn't be "it depends on the year." How many members will you have? This isn't a hard-and-fast number as much as a guideline. We fluctuate between seven and ten. Your numbers determine a lot about the group: voicing, amplification options, and expenses. Most importantly, what style music are you going to sing as your bread-and-butter? A cappella covers a wide range of options. Do you lean towards vocal jazz, straight pop, rock? While it is important to challenge your group with a variety of music, they must have a "home base." Your singers will spend time listening to and studying what they do most often, and you'll see this culture enhance your end product immensely.

Know Your Audience

The second step is closely related to the first. In order to determine how to be successful, you must consider who will be watching you most often, and who in that audience *counts* the most. Remember, you control the performance schedule of this group. Which of the following is most important to you?

» *Community Relations*: If you want to use this group as a way to build good will for your program within your community, you'll need to plan on singing for a lot of adult crowds. That means that your look, sound, and song selection can be contemporary, but not edgy. You'll have to have a more subdued tone in order to appeal to the public at large. Generally speaking, the masses like familiar and straight-up-the-middle.

» *Recruitment*: If your main purpose is to wow all your middle and high school students, you'll push to be the hippest-looking (and sounding) crew around. Sometimes adults might scratch their heads, but you're not worried about that. You just want young people to love you.

» *Fundraising*: This is closely related to *Community Relations*. At least in our neck of the woods, the folks who hire us are community groups like the Rotary Club, Lion's Club, Women's League, etc. We also do a fair number of appearances at local churches. Such groups often look for holiday appearances, so you'll need to have that repertoire in place to capitalize on those opportunities.

You can serve more than one of these functions at the same time, but having an awareness of how each function requires different strategies, music choices, and presentations will help you as you develop your identity. Because music selection is such a huge part of this planning, we'll give it more detail in Chapter 3.

Craft Your Image

Once you know who you are and what you are singing, the last step is to craft your image. Do you want to be perceived as edgy? Hip? Cool? Laid back? Jazzy?

Funny? Your image should always hold sway in the decision making process. Just because you are a high-school group doesn't mean you can't look professional. With today's technology, it should be relatively easy to develop a brand for your group. Get a logo, or at least a consistent typeface and color scheme for your group, and incorporate that into your materials. Your name, outfits, CD cover design, website, etc. should all express the same idea. This basic branding can be really effective in building the group's name/reputation in your community.

In conclusion, remember that as you work towards a group identity, there are aspects of your personality, age, and talent that are unchangeable. Don't just dream up a vision you can't achieve. Find what you do well naturally and exploit it like mad.

Summary

Begin with the end in mind:

» Define your group

» Know your audience

» Craft your image

» Consider how you will balance the following:

  • Community relations

  • Recruiting

  • Fundraising

» Find out what you can do well, and exploit that like crazy.

CHAPTER 2

The Audition

This chapter is devoted to designing the audition process for your group. There are many ideas listed here, but you certainly don't have to use them all. You can mix and match these ideas from year to year to keep your auditions fresh. However, there are a few things that you should probably do every cycle, and they are listed first.

Take a Survey

The majority of students who audition for your a cappella group will be singers who are already in your choir program. You may choose to expand your survey to include the band and/or orchestra. You're trying to estimate how many students are auditioning, and of what age and voice type. I'm sure I don't have to mention that the number of guys auditioning is usually at the top of most directors' minds.

Knowing how many students are auditioning will help you determine how to structure your process. If you have a lot of students, you can have auditions with cuts, then callbacks. If you don't have many students, you can probably just schedule everything for one night.

It's also important to know how many students are auditioning so you can steer the size of your group. If you're looking to have a group of 16, and only 18 students are coming to auditions, you could find yourself in an awkward situation. Groups like this should be selective to a degree, as a reward for great singers. It's hard to create that perception if everyone (or almost everyone) gets in. If you only have 18 auditionees, perhaps you'd be better off with a target group of 8-12.

Create an Audition Packet

It is important that everyone auditioning has the same information, so creating an audition packet is a must. That way, no one can say "I wasn't in class that day," or "I tried to come see you, but you weren't here." The packet should contain important details for the auditionees, as well as for their parents. It's hard to get much done without cooperative parents, and informed parents are happy parents.

Here are some things your audition packet should include:

» Your contact information (for questions)

» Audition dates and times

  • Date when the audition music will be available

  • Date(s) of actual audition(s)

» Audition requirements

  • How the process will run

  • What you're looking for during auditions

  • Who is eligible (some schools may choose to prohibit freshmen or students who are not in a music class)

» Schedule details

  • Rehearsals

  • Known concerts

  • Summer camp, if applicable

» Financial details

  • Outfit expectations (will the student purchase or will the program provide)

  • Cost to be in the group (if any), including when and to whom payment is due

» Information form (student will return to you)

  • Name

  • Grade

  • Address

  • Phone numbers and e-mail addresses (parents, student)

  • Grade estimates (I have found it extremely helpful to have an overview of each student's grades)

  • List of activities that could conflict with your schedule

  • Signature blanks (parents, student) to indicate the packet has been read and understood

Publicize

Your best hope of casting a great group is to get as many singers through the door as possible. It's a good idea to have your publicity start about a month before auditions. Create a poster that can be hung all over the school. Put reminders on your school's morning announcements. You could also make "table tents" to sit in the cafeteria at lunch. If you are accepting freshmen, don't forget to do the same at your middle schools so the eighth-graders get the word. Of course, announce it in class and get your fellow music teachers to do the same. Your poster should contain the audition dates and times, and where to pick up the audition packet (main office or similar place). If you have a website, put the address on the poster and link to the audition packet for download.

Distributing the Audition Music

If the singers have to learn specific music for auditions, it is best to ensure everyone has equal access. If you hand out audition music in class before the rest of the school has a chance to get it, you run the risk of perceived unfairness. The best solution is to post the music online, if it is something to which you have the rights. If it is a copyrighted song, you can put copies in the main office for sign-out. Let's say you buy 50 copies of your audition song. Number them 1-50 and have the students sign them out with the main office secretary. Post the notice that failure to return the music at auditions means the student's account will be charged. That way, you can keep track of the music in which you have invested. While your publicity might start about a month before the auditions, I recommend only giving the students a week to study their music. When the season starts, you'll need to know they can produce results in a reasonable amount of time.

Audition Stages (in no particular order)

The Golden Ticket

A quick way to find out who has the most promise in a field of auditionees is to have them sing a short 30-60 second solo a cappella, similar to the "Golden Ticket" stage of auditions on *American Idol*. This doesn't take much time, and quickly shows you who can sing in tune, present visually, and select a song that fits their voice. This is an especially good tool for arranging a first cut if you have a large field of singers. It's a safe bet that if you have 50-60 singers go through the "Golden Ticket" round, you will be able to cut a third of them right off the bat. If you don't want to make any cuts this soon, you'll at least have a working knowledge of who is at the front of the pack.

Learning a Sample Song

As you audition singers, the single most important factor is how well they can hold their own part. Even if they will eventually sing in a section of four voices, they can't be effective in a small group if they are leaning on others for help. Pick a song with relatively few voices (SATB, SSAA, or TTBB depending on your target group's gender) that the students can pick up one week prior to auditions. When they come to auditions, make four single-file lines—one for each voice part. After running through the song with everyone in the room to get the tempo down (and their nerves out), start with the front of the line. Have the first four sing, then rotate to the back. Make notes on a chart of the auditionees as you go. After everyone has gone through the line once, you can begin to create your own quartets to see which voices match. Remember that sometimes a singer can falter because others in their quartet were weak. Try them again in a stronger combination.

Making the Band . . .

This stage can tell you a lot about your singers. This challenge will reveal musicality, but also internal leadership and teamwork. I suggest splitting your auditionees into two groups, but you could split into three groups if your numbers are high.

Divide your singers in two groups, each containing half the available voice parts. That way, each group has the same voicing. Give each group a boom-box and a room of their own. Assign them one hour to come up with an a cappella arrangement of one of the songs on their CD. Let them know that they can do the whole song, or just a portion, but they have to make the best presentation possible. Remind them it's far better to do one verse and one chorus well than a complete song in shambles.

Each CD should contain a few popular songs that offer obvious opportunities for harmony. Make sure you have at least one with a male solo and one with a female solo.

Take your time over the next hour and move back and forth between the rooms. When you aren't in the room, the students will begin to shape their own internal dynamic. Leaders will emerge, and those who are timid will fade to the background. You'll get a sense of who is fearless in the face of a challenge and who is along for the ride.

Counterfeiting

A useful tool in a cappella is to create a variety of sounds. In order to create a sound, the singer must first hear and analyze the sound. One way to discover who can do this is to provide songs that are vocal models. Pick one song per voice type, preferably a jazz standard done by a singer with a lot of style. Ask each auditionee to perfectly copy the song chosen for their voice part, down to every slide, tonal change, and inflection. Not only are you testing their ears and their voice, but also their work ethic. How close to your idea of "perfect" is their version of "perfect?"

Clips with Your Existing Group

This is an exercise that I would suggest for an audition that has multiple stages. This should be the final stage. Make available sections of at least two songs that your group currently sings. Make sure one has a male solo and one has a female solo. Then, require your auditionees to learn one of the song sections that is **not** the solo. By doing this, you'll see how a new singer can hang with seasoned veterans, both vocally and visually. Will they pick up what the veterans are doing and follow along?

Posting Results

You'll want to post the results everywhere you publicized, so outside your choir room or the main office at the high school, and then perhaps outside the main office of the middle school(s). One thing I highly recommend is posting the results online. This way, each student can choose to handle the results in their own fashion. Before online posting, there was often a crowd of kids gathered around the choir room waiting for the results; it was tough to have some kids celebrating while others were disappointed. Online posting eliminates that phenomenon and allows everyone to check at their convenience, even from a smartphone if they are traveling at the time of posting.

I encourage you to post results the day following auditions, not the same night. It's always good to have some time to think on the process. If you tell your students the results will be up the same night, you've painted yourself into a corner time-wise.

Summary

These are just some suggestions for auditions. You can use as few or as many as you like, and change them from year to year to avoid the "what we always do is . . ." factor. Summarized below are two ways to approach the audition process.

Auditions in one night

» Golden Ticket

» Learning a sample song (music given out one week prior) OR

» Counterfeiting (music given out one week prior)

Auditions with callbacks

» First Night

  • Golden Ticket

  • Learning a sample song (music given out one week prior)

» Cuts with callback list posted

» Callbacks

  • Clips with your existing group OR

  • Learn a sample song OR

  • Making the band

CHAPTER 3

So What Do We Sing?

Once your a cappella group is up and running, you'll need some music. Some people will say "songs," "arrangements," "sheet music" or "charts," but they all mean the same thing. So . . . what do you sing? In this chapter, we'll explore not only where to get the sheet music, but also how to pick the songs and arrange them into a cohesive "set list" that keeps the audience entertained.

Where to Buy Music

There are three sources of music available to your group, each with their own strengths and weaknesses. They are (in no particular order):

Off-the-Rack Charts

Many publishers have arrangements ready for purchase. This is often the best "go-to" option, because they are inexpensive and ready to use. They also have been produced and edited by professionals who care about natural voice-leading, appropriate range, etc. While these arrangements might not bring "fireworks" to the table, you can spice them up at your discretion. If you have a really high tenor, for instance, you can add extra harmonies to show him off. If you have a very low bass, drop a couple notes down an octave for that "wow factor." When you consider what published charts to buy, you'll want to keep in mind the questions listed in the next section, *Custom Charts*. The same thought process applies here, but I have listed them in the next section, because it involves creating something from nothing rather than checking an existing product for fit.

Custom Charts

There are a lot of arrangers out there for hire. Like any business, there are some who are amazing and some who are, well . . . not. They all have different strengths and weaknesses, different price schedules, and different timetables. If you go down the road of commissioning custom charts, you really stand a chance of having an amazing result. You also stand the chance of wasting your money if you aren't careful. Here are some things to remember when commissioning an arrangement:

» *Who will be the soloist?* If you have a group with one voice per part, this is crucial, as the rest of the arrangement will be written accordingly. Even if you have multiple voices per part, the soloist will determine if you need to change the key of the song. Don't forget that you can take any song out there and make a "gender bender" out of it—a female song sung by a male or vice versa. If you have to transpose the song more than a half-step to accommodate your soloist, I would recommend a different song or a different soloist.

» *What is the voicing?* Always indicate to the arranger if you want the voicing to be SATB, SSAATTBB, etc. If you have a group of sixteen singers, you probably don't want SSSSAAAATTTTBBBB, but without any discussion, you might get just that. We'll talk more later about how to pick the difficulty of each song, which will help you determine how "thick" your arrangements should be.

» *What are the ranges of the singers?* Be specific. Include more than simple notes on the staff. If your sopranos have light, clear voices, say so. If you have an alto who can have a good sound doubling for a high tenor, say so. Arrangers not only craft the chart to fit ranges, but they use vocal color to help create interest in the music. Pitting timbres against each other can be very helpful, and you know these singers better than anybody.

» *What is your desired level of difficulty?* We want these songs to sound good to the audience, period. Making an arrangement difficult might sometimes be needed for a great musical effect, but sometimes it can just mean clutter. If you have a younger group, easier charts can breed confidence. Experienced, knowledgeable singers will often want something challenging to keep it fun for them. You will have to help your students with that balancing act. One other note: with a custom arrangement, you can say things like, "give the tougher parts to the tenors," "make sure the bass line is fairly simple," "our women have great vocal match, so please show that off," or "the second alto can do some vocal percussion if you want to add that somewhere."

» *Do you want a medley/mash-up?* A great bonus about custom charts is that the arranger can "mash-up" more than one song for you.

» *What are the terms?* Make sure you agree up front on the:

  • Price

  • Format (Finale, Sibelius, PDF, MIDI, hard copy, etc.)

  • Deadline for completion

» *Do you want a lift or a deconstruction?* A *lift* is an arrangement that mimics the sound of the original song as much as possible. It is like a transcription of the instrumentation with accommodations for being vocals only. A *deconstruction* is an arrangement done in a different speed and/or style than the original. Many examples of deconstructions can be found on *American Idol* when contestants try to make an existing song "their own."

- *Will you have exclusivity?* Arrangers sell commissioned music at one rate, then often sell their finished product again at a lower rate. If it matters to you, ask up front if this chart is being created just for you, and if so, how long you can keep exclusivity. Usually, one year is enough time, as groups are trying to ensure they don't sing the same arrangement as another group in competition.

- *Who handles the legal issues?* Make sure your arranger is taking care of this for you by securing permission and paying the licensing fees from the song's publisher. Since they do this much more often than you do, it shouldn't be a problem for them to keep you covered, but you must always make sure this aspect is handled legally.

Self-Arranging

With self-arranging, you arrange the song yourself or empower your students to get involved. This allows you to perfectly tailor each chart to your students' voices. If you get into rehearsal and something isn't working, you know exactly how to change it. In order to get your students involved, you could break down this daunting task into stages and assign them like weekly "homework."

» Pick the song

» Notate the melody

» Notate the bass line

» Figure out the chord changes

» Experiment in rehearsal (filling in the other "instrumentation" by creating rhythms within the harmony framework)

» Refine as much as you like

The benefits of self-arranging include the fact that it costs you no money (other than any licensing fee from the publisher), as well as that you are in complete control of the end product. If you get your students involved, you also have the opportunity to use this to supplement their classroom education. The drawbacks, however, include the time commitment (honestly, you may want to spend your time on other tasks to help your program) and the fact that your product might not turn out as well as what could be done by a professional.

How Much Music Do You Need?

If you plan to only sing on your own choir concerts, the answer is "however much you want." If you plan to do community engagements for hire, you'll need at least a 20–30 minute set. I feel confident about gigs once we have seven songs in place. Seven songs, plus applause and some talking with the audience, will yield a good package to present. There are, however, many people who would like 45–60 minutes of music, and then you'd have to double that number.

TIP: Learn some very easy music as "filler" for longer gigs. You don't have to sing the filler on your home concerts, but it can help you stretch when you have to sing longer for a private engagement.

How Do You Pick the Songs?

Here are some guidelines to how to pick songs for your set. To begin with, keep the following criteria in mind:

» *Lyrics.* G rated—always.

» *Age of audience.* We program multiple decades on purpose: newer songs for school events, older songs for Rotary Club gigs, etc. We are then completely covered for home concerts where high school students, parents, and grandparents are all in the audience. They all get to hear something they like.

» *Familiarity.* It sometimes feels "cheap," but audiences love the familiar. We get more mileage out of Stevie Wonder's "Signed, Sealed, Delivered," than we would from "I Wish." You can see the crowd have the "oh, yeah" moment when their faces say, "I know that song."

» *Difficult does not always equal better.* My kids like to sing charts that are hard, because it is challenging for them. What they sometimes forget is that we need to fill as much as an hour, and learning that much difficult music can be exhausting. Consider each song as an investment. While I love a certain, particularly difficult, arrangement of the National Anthem, we stopped singing it because it had a low return on investment. When singing the anthem for the Friday night football game on one microphone broadcast over the stadium public address system, those really cool, thick chords didn't mean squat. An easier arrangement got the same crowd response and took much less rehearsal time, giving us more time to put into our main performance package.

» *Get some mileage out of "double-dip" songs.* There are some songs that are so great, they are covered by more than one artist in more than one era. "Some Kind of Wonderful" is an outstanding song originally written by John Ellis. It later became a hit for Grand Funk Railroad in 1975, then again for Huey Lewis and the News in 1994. In 2003, it was covered in a soul style by Joss Stone, and then later that decade by Michael Buble. Peforming a song like that can connect with many age groups at the same time.

Once you've familiarized yourself with these criteria, it's time to get down to the nitty-gritty of picking songs. Here are some topics to help you get focused:

» *Who will be the soloist?* Many groups pick songs first and then audition the soloists afterward. I suggest you reverse that process. Identify your great soloists, and then pick songs that will show them off. If you have a big group, you can certainly still hold auditions (and you might get some great surprises), but at least you'll have a starting point.

» *Remember the tempi.* Too much of anything gets boring. You'll need some exciting up-tunes, some medium-speed swing or groove songs, and at least one solid ballad. That way, you can provide variety and flow to your set.

» *Music through the ages.* I don't think any high school group would choose to be a group that only sings songs from 1965–1967. Why, then, would you only sing songs on the radio today? I ask my singers to bring in song ideas from different eras: 50s & 60s, 70s, 80s, 90s–2000, and today. Try to have a variety of eras in your show. It will allow you to connect with a wider audience and will expand your students' horizons.

» *What styles?* There are a lot of styles of popular music. You have to remember that we are trying to sound authentic, so make sure you choose carefully. If you want to sing rock, you can sing rock—but you might not be able to pull off Aerosmith with Steven Tyler's gravelly screaming vocals. If you don't have a soulful soloist, don't try to sing soul or R&B. If you pick a song that has a strong high tenor line, don't forget that you could make it a "gender bender" for a stellar alto.

» *Who gets input?* This is a point of much controversy. I let my students have input on song selection. Notice I did not say that I let my students pick the songs. You can handle this however you like, either giving them all the control or by picking everything yourself. Here's how we do it.

   • Each of my students is required to bring me a CD with the top five songs they think they can sing well, covering multiple eras.

   • I listen to all the songs and provide feedback. If I think a student has made solid choices, I will pick one of their songs to go on to the "finals."

   • If the student didn't have a great first round, I might suggest to them some songs I think would work better, and let them repeat the process.

   • We bring the "finalists" together and listen to them as a group.

   • I give every student one "veto" card for the whole year. There are too many songs in the world for us to spend a whole year with a singer hating a song every second, but they must understand how to really use good judgement before they speak up. If they pull out the veto card, I know it's going to be a real rub all year.

   • After all that input, I make the final decision.

- While this sounds like a lot of work, I guarantee you that taking sufficient time at the start of your season to pick music that everyone enjoys is crucial. You'll probably be working together on it *all year*, which is unlike the performance cycle of concert choirs. If you're going to live with this music for a year, it's best that you all like it.

Summary

» Use a combination of off-the-rack, custom, and self-arranged charts to fill out your set according to your budget, vocal needs, rehearsal schedule, and performance needs.

» Consider soloists, tempi, styles, and eras to create a varied set.

» Work with your students to get the best selection of song options.

CHAPTER 4

How to Structure Your Rehearsal

A retired engineer from General Motors once told me, "It doesn't matter what you do, only that you plan to do it." He went on to explain that many perceived bad habits are seen in that negative light when they have simply happened, rather than been planned. Take, for instance, sleeping in. Sleeping in can sometimes be a healthy indulgence, if planned for in advance. Sleeping in several days a week "just because it happened" is a problem. Taking a nap, watching TV, monitoring Facebook, playing video games, and other such perceived "time wasters" are considered such because they keep us from our plans. How many people plan their Facebook time? "15 minutes before bed, and that's all . . ." More often they say, "Well, I was just Facebooking and lost track of the time."

Towards that end, it is crucial that you plan your rehearsals right down to the minute. That is not to say that you cannot alter your rehearsal schedule as it evolves—far from it. You should constantly evaluate your timeline as it progresses. But the schedule should be designed with the achievement of musical goals in mind, providing constant awareness. If you run long in one segment, you'll find that you fight harder to get back on track in the next. You'll also identify patterns. If every one of your rehearsal segments is running long, you'll need to rehearse more efficiently or make a more realistic schedule next time. Having a schedule also provides incentive for students to stay on task. There is always the unspoken drive to get done early, both for the feeling of achievement and the joy of adding in a fun bonus in any remaining time.

Your rehearsal structure should contain some consistent components but the specifics, and allotted time of each component should change from rehearsal to rehearsal in order to provide continued interest to the singers. Here are of some of the major components from which you can draw when constructing your rehearsal plan.

Rehearsal Components

Warm-ups

Warm-ups come in infinite variety. A common trap into which a cappella groups fall is not warming up their voices. Runners always stretch before a practice, and so should you. Good vocal pedagogy is good vocal pedagogy. Always begin with the tried-and-true warm-ups you use with all of your groups to ensure your singers are singing healthily. A good general guideline of how to structure warm-ups includes:

» Stretching to awaken the body

» Breathing exercises to heighten awareness

» Unison mid-range exercises

» Slow expansion of the range, difficulty, and number of parts in exercises

» Chordal exercises to sharpen tuning

The Kickstart

A great thing to do after warm-ups is run through a favorite song. This should be a song that everyone feels confident while performing. This is not supposed to be everyone's favorite song, because sometimes such songs are not in very good musical shape. This should be a song that sings consistently well, in addition to being fun to sing. Consider this as "calibrating" your singers for rehearsal. Starting with a fun, solid song gets students excited and ready for more.

Progress Check

The end of each rehearsal should contain practice goals for all singers. Therefore, the beginning of each rehearsal should contain run-throughs of those songs to check for progress. Restate the goals from last practice: "Last time we met, we said we would work on X, Y, and Z. Let's see how well we did before we get into our rehearsal." A progress check will let you know if you need to send a song into sectionals or send it into *the cycle* (explained later), as well as if you need to shorten/lengthen the time given to this particular song in your rehearsal plan.

Sectionals

You can get a lot done with sectionals, if they are handled correctly. Since there is only one of you, you'll need section leaders or a student director to share the load. In a mixed group, you could split up into four sections (Soprano, Alto, Tenor, Bass) or simply split guy/girl. Sectionals are great for those times you just have to hammer out a lot of notes, and they build confidence by allowing singers to work out the kinks in front of a smaller audience. Be careful, though. I suggest to you here (and will expound elsewhere) that your rehearsals **not** take too much time for note-pounding. You have many jobs as the director, and note-pounding should be the least of them.

The Cycle

When I say, *the cycle,* I'm referring to a set pattern of how to rehearse one song. Each song in a rehearsal gets its own *cycle,* and though the length will be different for each one, you will consistently use the rehearsal techniques listed in the other chapters to:

» Restate current musical goals for this song.

» Break down the song by sections (in reference to form) and by part grouping ("Let's hear whomever has the bell chord . . .") to polish the components.

» Rebuild the song after having improved the individual pieces. Do this one section at a time, gluing more sections together until you are running the song.

» Run through the song to make a recording/capture (so that you have a record of improvement against which to practice).

» Set goals for your next rehearsal for this song.

Business Meeting

Because your group will have non-musical items to discuss, such as outfits, gig dates, rehearsal changes, trips, fees, etc. it is important to make time for a business meeting inside your rehearsal. It doesn't have to take long, but this must be a habit for your singers. If you don't have one each rehearsal, students usually start forgetting important information. Business meetings reinforce the culture that each singer has a responsibility to the group, both musically and administratively.

Recording / Evaluation

Recording is an immensely beneficial tool for any performing group. While *the cycle* contains time to record performances for future study, take the time to do a recording that the group can evaluate immediately during rehearsal. This doesn't have to happen every rehearsal, but it is a good tool to use on occasion. When students know they are being recorded and evaluated, they perform differently. This provides a very positive, yet unspoken pressure to perform well.

Running the Set

As a performance gets closer, sometimes you just need to run your whole set without stopping, complete with logistics such as making your entrance, singing, talking, and exiting. A great thing to do as you near a performance is to videotape a set, watch the video, discuss it, and then run it again.

The Closer

This is the opposite of the *kickstart.* Select the song that the students have made the farthest advances on during rehearsal and close with it, so that they end with a feeling of huge accomplishment.

Sample Rehearsals

This sample is arranged for a two-hour rehearsal, assuming the group meets after school hours. It is only one variation on a theme; you can adapt this sample as you see fit. In each rehearsal, I would suggest starting with the song that needs the most rehearsal. This generally makes the group feel better, as if the toughest task is out of the way. Also, if you need a little longer on your most challenging piece, you can adjust your rehearsal accordingly.

Early in the Learning Process

» Warm-ups	10 minutes
» The Kickstart	5 minutes
» Sectionals	20 minutes
» The Cycle – Song 1	20 minutes
» Break	5 minutes
» Business Meeting	5 minutes
» The Cycle – Song 2	15 minutes
» The Cycle – Song 3	15 minutes
» The Cycle – Song 4	15 minutes
» Goal Setting	5 minutes
» The Closer	5 minutes
» Dismissal (end on time)	

Standard Rehearsal

» Warm-ups	10 minutes
» The Kickstart	5 minutes
» Progress Check	10 minutes
» The Cycle – Song 1	30 minutes
» Break	5 minutes
» Business Meeting	5 minutes
» The Cycle – Song 2	20 minutes
» Recording Evaluation	10 minutes
» The Cycle – Song 3	15 minutes
» Goal Setting	5 minutes
» The Closer	5 minutes
» Dismissal (end on time)	

Nearing Performance /Dress Rehearsal

» Warm-ups	10 minutes
» Run the Set	20 minutes
» Evaluation of Set (video)	30 minutes
» Break	5 minutes
» Business Meeting	5 minutes
» Tweak Problems in Set	20 minutes
» Break	5 minutes
» Run the Set	20 minutes
» Goal Setting	5 minutes
» Dismissal (end on time)	

Auxillary Rehearsals

Your group will certainly improve with each regularly scheduled rehearsal; however, they will grow much faster if you add in some very easy, enjoyable extras that serve as team-spirit builders.

The Quick Run

A challenge for any performing group is keeping older repertoire up to snuff. Rehearsal time is precious and often focused on the development of new material. In order to keep the older songs sharp, I suggest *the quick run*. All you need is five to ten minutes at a time, a couple times each week to do a performance run of one to three songs. Let's say you have an eight-song repertoire. Maybe your schedule looks like this:

» Week 1

- Tuesday after school: Song 1 and Song 2

- Thursday after school: Song 3 and Song 4

» Week 2

- Tuesday after school: Song 5 and Song 6

- Thursday after school: Song 7 and Song 8

My favorite thing to do (if possible) is to have the group meet on their way out of the building to sing one song every day. Most students have a few minutes after school before they leave for home. If not, there may be a chance to get together for just five minutes on the way into school homeroom, or maybe your students all share the same lunch period. In my case, school ends at 3:05, so the *quick run* starts at 3:10. Everyone who can make it does a performance run of one song. If a member can't make it due to another commitment, we perform without them. If too many can't make it, we skip that day. Still, it works on most days. Not only are the singers keeping their repertoire fresh, they also have a chance to touch base with each other.

Student-Run Rehearsals

One of the best things for a group is student-run rehearsals. I credit these rehearsals with the success of my group, Eleventh Hour. Each week, we rehearse once for three hours with myself directing. Then the students have another three-hour rehearsal on a different night, completely by themselves.

Student-run rehearsals allow the singers to experiment with new sounds, new visual plans, and other performance ideas. Students are inherently creative, but sometimes will not bring forth ideas in front of the director, for fear of wasting time or being wrong. When students have time in which they can experiment, they become fearless. Ideas pour out of them, which they should assess, in order to bring you only the very best. When you next rehearse together, you'll have some new performance options to consider.

Student-run rehearsals are also a great time for the group to solidify performance goals from your last meeting together. Use a student director to keep everyone on track. When the students take ownership, their performance level can greatly increase. One of the goals of music education is to develop students' independence, and student-run rehearsals can help this immensely.

Practice vs. Rehearsal

One thing I do each year is to define these two words for all my singers. *Rehearsal* is what we do together, as a group. *Practice* is what each singer must do on their own time to be ready for rehearsal. While I can't expect every student in my program to be independent, I do expect this of my singers in Eleventh Hour. We do not "bang out notes" in rehearsal unless we have an emergency of some sort, like the need to learn a specific song very quickly for a special gig. You are a talented director, and have much more to offer students than playing notes. With the technology that exists today, including music notation software, midi playback, and digital recorders, any student has the opportunity to practice notes on their own. Make this a rule and stick with it. It will pay off tenfold as your season progresses. The difference between practice and rehearsal is so important it has its own chapter later in this handbook.

Summary

» Plan your work; work your plan—account for every minute.

» Set goals for each rehearsal and regularly check your progress.

» Rehearsals don't have to be long—even 10 minutes can be helpful.

» Students can and should do work without you present. It gives them ownership and enables creativity.

» Learn the difference between *practice* and *rehearsal*.

CHAPTER 5

REHEARSAL TECHNIQUES

❝I miss teaching. I don't miss the games.
I don't miss the tournament.
I miss the daily practices.❞

—Coach John Wooden

The heart and soul of any group comes from the practices. This is where the magic happens, where students learn new material and hone their skills. It's why teachers teach. Like all teachers, I enjoy "watching the light bulb go off" more than anything. That's why I love a cappella groups. I have yet to find a musical outlet that allows so much room for student empowerment. In these small ensembles, each person not only has to know their part, but perform it with personality, style, and ownership.

In this chapter, we will discuss strategies to make your a cappella group perform better. There are idiosyncrasies to this style that need addressing to get maximum results. Some of these strategies are essential, and some are just fun techniques to add variety to your routine. They are presented in no particular order.

Divide and Conquer

A cappella often creates textures by pitting different groups of singers against each other. Sometimes arrangements have a few voices singing whole-note chords while other voices have complex rhythmic sounds. Arrangers do this to maintain tonal stability while keeping rhythmic motion alive. Other times, all the voices might work together, either in a bell chord pattern or in complete homophony.

When we direct choirs, we are asking all the singers to match: match each other, match vowels, match posture, match cutoffs, match our modeling, and so on. Of course, a cappella groups have to match, too. But what do they have to match? That depends on what's going on in the arrangement, and it can change from phrase to phrase.

Let's say you're performing a song that imitates a horn line. The horns have to match each other, but they don't have to match the bass. They don't have to match other parts that imitate guitars. Sure, they have to be rhythmically precise, in tune and musical, but the whole group doesn't have to match (unless it is a homophonic section). In fact, when representing a band, they should not match.

Because of this construction, the most important thing to remember about rehearsing an a cappella group is the old adage "divide and conquer." Examine your arrangement, and make sure you have a mental map of what is going on, section by section. As the director, you have to know the form of the song. You also have to exploit differences between sections to provide contrast and interest. A good arrangement has built-in components to help you, so consider rehearsing each different texture differently.

It will be tempting to rehearse the whole group all the time. While that keeps all your singers singing more often, it probably isn't the best way to maximize your results. Examine who is grouped together, and rehearse them separately. Any voices grouped with the same rhythms should work together. While you are doing this, have your other singers listen and be ready to offer input. This is also a great time to check your "syllable sounds." For instance, if you are doing a section of guitar sounds, you can ask each student to create their own sound and sing it individually. Take a survey of the group to find out what they think sounds best. Then have the singers of that "group" match that sound. You have now not only found your "target sound," but have empowered the students to be creative. You have also trained their ears and let them know that their opinion matters.

After you have rehearsed each section, lay them on top of each other. You'll then discover if the "target" sounds of each section are too similar or too disparate. Just as a well-constructed recipe has a balance of flavors, you'll need a balance of sound. Too many sounds that are similar can sound like a wall of noise, and thus diminish the effects of intentional homophony when they arise.

Next, rehearse the rhythm section (bass and drums) alone, or with the soloist. Make sure that they are singing with a good feel for the groove of the song. Many people call this being "in the pocket." Imagine catching a baseball in a well-conditioned glove. There is a "pocket" that helps trap the ball after catching to keep it in place. If you sing "in the pocket" of the beat, you'll stay together better. Use body movement or even walk to the beat to help this happen.

Finally, put all your sections back together for a run-through. Make sure that each section is aware of how they play off one another and how each fits into the rhythmic pocket. The results should speak for themselves.

There's A Little Drummer in Everyone . . .

Many a cappella groups get too dependent on the fact that, unlike concert choirs, they have a drummer in the band. You can tell this is happening when the singers rarely move, look at the drummer a lot, or ask for more vocal percussion in the monitor mix. While the drummer has to be in time, they are not in charge of keeping time. If anyone is in charge of keeping time, it's the bass part, but even that is a bit of a crutch. That's why we say, "There's a little drummer in everyone." Each singer is responsible for keeping time, or else they'll have difficulty holding things together when the going gets rough. How can you help all those internal drummers grow strong?

Try doing run-throughs of the song with no vocal percussion at all. Start the group singing against a metronome to keep the beat, then occasionally turn the volume down for a few bars. When you turn the volume back up, are they still in time? Once the singers are more secure, you can increase the length of time without the metronome. Keep testing them. Finally, start the song with the metronome, then turn it off. Record the performance. When you play it back, have the singers tap along with the recording to see if they make it all the way through without adjusting. Everyone will feel the variance if it occurs.

Another way to test the "inner drummer" is to start the song in performance position, and then begin moving all around the room. Make the singers move in all directions, not even looking at each other. They'll really have to listen to stay in tune, but mostly they'll hang on to their internal beat. Assign a point in the song where they come back together, and watch their faces light up when they are still on track.

Using Recorders

The most powerful tool a young singer can have is a personal recorder. It could be a dedicated recorder, or even one of the many applications available on today's smartphones and mp3 players. It's a great way to capture information at rehearsal for practice at home. Here are some ways to use recording technology to your advantage.

Swapping Performances

Have each student hold their own recorder as they perform a song. You'll probably want to do just a portion, stop, listen back to ensure the level is good, then start over to get the whole song. Perform the whole song while each student records themselves. Assign them the task of going home and reviewing their recording, making notes on what they did well and what they can improve. After doing so, they should swap recordings with another person in the group and do the same. Bring both assessments back to rehearsal and talk through them. It is eye-opening to discover the difference in evaluation. We often get too close to our own performances, and even miss our own mistakes. After all, no one intentionally tries to do something wrong.

Capturing the Target Run-through

During rehearsal, you probably spend a lot of time trying to add value to your performance . . . maybe you worked very hard on your volume plan or getting your rhythms in the pocket; maybe you changed something in the arrangement to better suit your group; maybe you worked extra hard to get an authentic sound for an instrument. Once you feel it is as good as it will get for the night, have every singer make a recording of the group performing the song all the way through. That new and better version of the song is now your digital roadmap. Students will hear their own improvement, and have every reason to remember what you did in rehearsal.

Each time they listen to the three-minute song, they'll be reminded of what they improved and hear what they need to improve for next time.

One Take

Assign your singers the challenge of recording a song (or section of a song) on which you are currently working. They should do it at home, outside rehearsal time. They are to hand just one "take" in to you for your review. They are allowed to try as many times as they want at home until they are satisfied, but they are to only deliver one "take." This starts a fantastic cycle of self-evaluation, as the students transition from "Wow, that's not so great" to "That was really good, but I can do better" to "I'm not turning this in until it is perfect!"

Model Voices

If you have a group in which there is more than one singer per voice part, spend some time listening to each singer sing. For any given song (or section of a song), you'll find that one singer is making the best sound in their section. Have them vocally model and the rest of the section match them. In a different section or texture, it might be a different student. You'll often find that one of your singers has the purest vowels, but another singer has the best style. You can use them at different times to great effect, or ask the students to incorporate both qualities at once if they can.

Over time, students will work hard to be the "model voice." You'll also have a target at which each singer can aim. I can be a great baritone model, but have a much tougher time at soprano. No matter what voice part you are, you're not all of them.

The Irresistible Force and the Immovable Object

There are two enormous components to great singing: rhythm and pitch. A group who can sing in time with each other while holding their tuning against a solid key center has most of what it needs to be successful. It is a strong foundation on which to build.

The *irresistible force* is tempo. When performing properly, it should be more difficult to "fall out of time" than to "stay on the beat."

The *immovable object* is the tonal center. When everyone tunes against the tonal center (or "do"), mistakes are less common and easier to fix. Imagine a chord is out of tune (I know, hard to imagine, right?). Adjustments must be made quickly, so the best chance of improvement comes from adjusting your part to the tonal center first. Otherwise, every singer would have to wonder which other singers are out of tune, and to whom they should adjust. A solid tonal center means everyone has a home base.

It can be immensely helpful to rehearse against a metronome for tempo and a tone generator for pitch. You can do one or the other, or both at the same time. In order to keep the singers from depending too much on muscle memory, you could intentionally change the tempo to be faster or slower. You could sing the song up or down a half-step. You should not only train for performances to go right, but you should be ready to deal with what happens when things go wrong.

Remember the old question, "What happens when an irresistible force meets an immovable object?" Answer: musical magic.

Get in Shape for the Stage

A common problem with performers is that they struggle adapting from rehearsal to the performance stage. They feel comfortable in rehearsal, but when the lights are on and hundreds of people are staring at them, they get an adrenaline rush. Then what happens? There's often a shortness of breath and a rush of energy. In order to simulate this effect, I suggest you take it to the max for your singers. Have them wear shoes appropriate for running to rehearsal and let them know what's going to happen. Have the pitch pipe ready. Then have them run a few laps around the school to get them winded. When they arrive back at your rehearsal space, there's no resting. Blow the pitch pipe and go. They are not allowed to stop performing. Granted, this type of fatigue goes way beyond what's going to hit them on stage, but it will raise their awareness (and determination to succeed) quite a bit.

We Are Experiencing Technical Difficulties

If you sing with any kind of amplification, this is a great exercise. There are many ways to try it. The big picture is trying to get your students used to dealing with technical glitches in a performance. Here are some things you can do to see how well your singers adapt:

» Wait until the song begins, then kill their monitors.

» Randomly turn off one microphone. See what the singers will do. If you kill a really crucial microphone, like the soloist, bass, or vocal percussionist, will they trade with each other (thus sharing backing vocals on a microphone)? Will they just look around and give up? After doing this, let them know what you think is the best option.

» Kill everything, as if the power just went out. Will the singers move on stage to ensure the audience gets great "raw" sound?

Houston, We Have a Problem . . .

Another good "think-on-your-feet" exercise is to internally sabotage a performance run-through to see how the students will handle adverse situations on stage. You need to coordinate this in advance with one of your singers so that it looks like an accident, then you can let the group in on the secret later. Some examples:

» Have the pitch blower blow the key of the song up or down one half-step.

» Have the vocal percussionist, bass, or soloist get caught up in a "coughing fit" that lasts a bit too long. Will the group keep going? If you do this for the soloist, can they motion to someone else in the group to take over?

» Have the soloist skip a verse or chorus to see if the group will follow them.

Sing in Circles

No, I don't mean stand in a circle. When I say *sing in circles* I am referring to the underlying pulse of a song. Imagine a song in 4/4 time. Take your hand and make four circles in the air—one for each quarter note. Sing the song while making a pulse every time you hit the bottom of the circle (on the beat). Now make bigger circles that match each half note. Sing the same song again matching those pulses. What next? You guessed it—one big circle per measure. You should have three distinctly different feels if you did it correctly. Remember that singing "circles" creates momentum. Think of riding a looping roller coaster. The coaster doesn't go around the loop at the same consistent speed. It slows a bit at the top, then accelerates back towards the bottom. Picking the right circle pattern creates energy toward the pulse of the song and maintains momentum in your phrases.

Looping

A modern musical phenomenon is that of *looping*. Simply put, looping is an ostinato pattern. It is a small chunk of music that seamlessly repeats over and over. Looping can be heard in techno-music, video games, commercials, radio, TV bumper music, and more.

When you are rehearsing, you'll often find that the toughest part of a song may be just a few measures. It might be a bell chord that repeats throughout the song, or a particularly difficult key-change between sections of the song. It might be a phrase ending where all the voices go homophonic for two bars.

Whatever the challenging material might be, a great rehearsal technique is *looping*.

» Tell your singers that you're going to loop a section of the music. (Make sure you explain the *looping* process.)

» Let them know the problem they are having, and the end result you desire.

» Demonstrate how you will do the loop. I suggest that you build in some period of rest before restarting the loop in which you can interject some instruction.

» Choose who will rehearse the loop first, and let the group know that anyone can be called in or out of the looping each time. This will keep them all listening and alert, thinking in advance of how to do well when it is their turn. Any changes you make to the music must be applied by all who enter the loop.

» Begin looping. Let's say you are doing a two-bar phrase (eight counts). Plan eight counts of singing and eight counts of feedback. In this illustration the counting represents singing, while the words represent the feedback between cycles:

- 1-2-3-4-5-6-7-8

- Do it again, but this time much brighter.

- 1-2-3-4-5-6-7-8

- Add the altos this time.

- 1-2-3-4-5-6-7-8

- Altos, make the B♮ higher.

- 1-2-3-4-5-6-7-8

- Good job altos, now add the tenors.

- 1-2-3-4-5-6-7-8

- Everyone purify their vowels.

- 1-2-3-4-5-6-7-8

- Great job, now add the drums.

- 1-2-3-4-5-6-7-8

- Now everyone accent the downbeats.

- 1-2-3-4-5-6-7-8

- Awesome! That's what we want!

» Point out the benefits of looping to your students:

- Everyone has to listen constantly and think proactively.

- You get many attempts in a short amount of time. Let's say our example above was at the tempo 120. In just 1:04, we had eight run-throughs, with feedback. Not bad.

Other Miscellaneous Tidbits

Remember that all singers have natural tendencies to overcome, especially those with little experience. As you rehearse, you'll notice that most singers are afraid to go "whole-hog" for fear of making a noticeable mistake. That can lead to bland, static sound and a lot of "sameness" in performance. Consider the following:

» High energy, faster songs can get frantic. Approach them with control and keep the rhythmic pocket in mind. The more rhythmic a song is, the more you'll have to think overall phrase shape.

» Slower, "cooler" songs trick students into giving less energy. Laid back songs actually require more energy, not less, but that energy must live under the surface. Imagine a duck gliding along the lake, but its unseen legs are paddling like crazy.

» Loud is not the answer, unless you are trying to be louder. Many times, singers will respond to requests for energy, diction, articulation, and even tuning by simply getting louder. Avoid this at all costs.

» If it sounds corny, it is. Many students will make an instrument sound and then stick with it forever, thinking that is the best sound they can make. In reality, it might be the best sound they can make just then, but over time, their mastery should grow. They should continually experiment with new, improved sounds.

» Cross the line. If you are trying to make something rhythmic, make it more and more rhythmic until it become obnoxious, then back it off a notch. If something is supposed to crescendo, hyper-crescendo. Most of the time, your singers won't know how far is "far enough" until they've gone "too far." They'll never know where the line is until they've crossed it.

Summary

The style of music you are rehearsing is different than your concert repesrtoire, so you must think outside the rehearsal box in which we often live as choir directors. Experiment—there are no wrong answers. You must keep your rehearsal mentally focused, but full of musical abandon. Make big mistakes and try many options as you quickly sort through the results to find what you most want to hear on stage. Then capture that result through writing and recording. Practice it before the next rehearsal to ingrain the changes you have made.

CHAPTER 6

TURKEY BACON
OR "HOW TO SOUND AUTHENTIC"

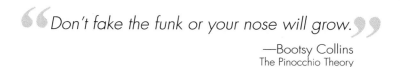

Don't fake the funk or your nose will grow.

—Bootsy Collins
The Pinocchio Theory

When a cappella was just getting started at my school, we had a guest artist come to town for student workshops and a concert. Their name was The Fault Line and they had just come off a successful run on the television show *America's Got Talent*.

The Fault Line wanted to establish themselves as the consummate "rock band" of a cappella, and they were doing a great job. They used a lot of electronic effects in their act, but they would have been worthless without an authentic musical style, provided by great mouth sounds going into the microphones.

Our kids started their workshop by singing a funk tune in a mostly non-funky way. After the song was over, one of The Fault Line guys said, "I feel like I just ate turkey bacon and all I can think is, 'This isn't bacon. It's close, but the fact that it's *almost* bacon makes me upset. All I want is bacon!'"

That is how you must approach your music. You can't be *almost* anything. You can't be *almost* grooving, *almost* rocking, *almost* funky, *almost* cool, or *almost* jazzy. You have to go all the way. You have to be bacon—not turkey bacon.

This is easier said than done, but it isn't as hard as you might think, either. You're a good musician and your singers probably are good musicians, too. They know what's lame and what is real. Your ear will not lie to you if you listen, so follow the plan below and you'll be more authentic.

Your Plan of Attack

Provided you have an arrangement, you really only have to deal with a few basics to get up and running. They are:

» Listen to the original

» Know the form

» Work out your syllables

» Deal with the rhythm section (bass and drums)

Listen to the Original

The first thing to do is to listen to the original version of the song. It might be more accurate to say the "iconic" version of the song: the one that audiences are most likely to know. For example, "Hound Dog" was originally done by Big Mama Thornton, but it is an iconic Elvis song.

Listen a few times. The first time, listen to the big picture. Then take a few turns mentally isolating different musical elements of the song: bass, drums, backing vocals, guitar part, horn line, etc. Mentally catalog the musical elements. Then listen while following along in the arrangement. Answer these questions:

» Is it in the same key?

» Is it a "lift" arrangement (meaning a near-transcription of the band's parts) or is it more creatively done?

» Is the arrangement clearly intended to follow the iconic interpretation, or is it "deconstructed?"

  • Deconstructed arrangements are those that are done in a completely different style. Examples include Michael Buble performing "Can't Buy Me Love" as a big band chart or Harry Connick, Jr. performing "If I Only Had a Brain" as a piano ballad.

» What do the vocal lines represent?

  • If you are singing a 3-part "horn line" you will approach your singing differently than if you are singing a rhythm guitar lick.

  • How should the solo sound? (Crucial if trying to be authentic.)

Know Your Form

Now that you have a mental map of the components in your arrangement, it's time to make sure you work through the form of the song with your group. It can be tempting to dive in and start "banging out notes," but don't do it! Before you begin anything, make sure your group understands the form of the song. To do that, you must:

» Break the song into sections

» Determine the character of each section (especially for the drummer)

» Make appropriate transitions between sections

» Hit the anchor points

First, establish a vocabulary with your singers. While you can use any terms you like, some common terms include:

» *Intro*: The opening of the song. This is often just instrumental, setting the style and beat of the song before the soloist's entrance.

» *Verse*: Roughly corresponding to a poetic stanza, each verse has the same musical structure, but different lyrics, carrying forward the story of the song.

» *Pre-Chorus*: A small bit of music that connects a verse to the chorus, not substantial enough to be a bridge.

» *Chorus* (or *Hook*): The "ear worm" of the song, identified as the part where everyone sings along.

» *Bridge*: A section that differs from the verse and chorus in harmonic construction. Bridges provide interest and relief from repetition either through instrumental music or lyrics.

» *Solo*: Feature for one instrument or voice.

» *Break*: Similar to a solo, but in a break, everyone one else (other than the soloist) drops out. What we think of as a drum solo is often really a "drum break."

» *Collision*: A short section of music in which two different melodies or themes overlap one another. It is mostly used in fast-paced music to create tension and drama. For example, during a chorus late in the song, the composer may interject musical elements from the bridge.

» *Outro*: A short ending section to the song, sometimes a vamp based on the chorus.

» *Ad lib*: A performer using song material in a freely interpreted fashion.

Write your form vertically down the left-hand side of a piece of paper. You are beginning to make a grid that will become the map to your interpretation.

Once each section of the song has been determined, you can write in the measure numbers next to the labels. After that, write in other notes that will tell your ensemble how to sing that section. You can make as many columns as you want in your grid. Some options are: dynamics, tone quality, articulation, instrumentation, and "cherries." You surely know what most of those labels mean, but "cherries" stands for little extras that stand out in each section (like cherries on a sundae). It might be a short section of harmony, a drum solo, or a low bass note. "Cherries" are anything that provide a quick "wow" moment in your performance. If you don't have any when you first make your form map, create some as your rehearsals unfold.

Now, your form map is in place, and it is easy to see the differences between sections. The next step is to decide how to transition between these sections. A great example is moving from a *verse* into a *chorus*. The chorus almost always receives a notch up in intensity and volume—it's the most memorable part of the song. If we are moving from *mezzo-forte* in the verse to *forte* in the chorus, what's the best way to do that? Based on the arrangement, does it make more sense to *crescendo* the last phrase of the verse, leading into the downbeat of the chorus, or just "flip the switch" on that downbeat, immediately getting louder?

The downbeat that begins each section is an "anchor point" in the music. Think of these anchor points as poles holding up a tent. The bigger a tent is or the more elaborate the shape a tent has, the more tent poles you have to hold it up. Imagine a tent with only one tent pole. Not so wonderful, is it? So it goes with music—you must have these musical anchor points in order to keep your interest propped up. By giving each section of the song an identifiable character, and by transitioning well (hitting anchor points), you will create forward momentum that keeps the audience interested. It keeps your singers interested, too! (If anyone in the group is bored, they will be boring to the audience.)

Remember to always sing with a plan. A bad plan can be improved, but the lack of a plan will always lead to sameness. Sameness leads to boredom, and in turn, boredom leads to failure.

How to Handle Syllables

This is probably the most crucial part of your a cappella existence. Once rehearsal starts, most singers immediately become concerned with tuning and right notes (as they should). However, to be successful as an a cappella group, you must have a command of singing syllables. A cappella syllables allow us to create instrumental sounds with our mouths. The four steps to syllable mastery are:

- » Free yourself from language

- » Remember that syllables are physical guidelines

- » Listen—your ear is king

- » Experiment

One of the biggest traps directors and singers fall into is worrying about what is printed on the page. *Yes*, you should get the right words, notes, rhythms, dynamic markings, etc. However, in the world of contemporary pop a cappella, the arrangement is sometimes considered a starting point—a framework. Consider the best chefs in the world. Do they use recipes? Sure they do. Still, they taste all along the way. They adjust. That's why phrases like "season to taste" exist. You must be a musical chef. As you determine how you will interpret this music, you must season to taste.

How will you sing a backing vocal line that says, "Jum-di-jum-di-jum-di-jum-jum?" In the syllables "Jen jen jo-do," how should you sing "Jen?" Like the first syllable of **Jen**nifer? What would happen if you sang it **gin**? What about just **jn**?

Free Yourself from Language

I can't recall where this quote came from, but I think it was from a barbershop singer: "We don't sing in English; we sing in Singlish. " The thrust of this quote is that singers must alter pronunciation and enunciation to produce a solid stream of in-tune singing. This could include sustaining voiced consonants or deliberately timing the turn of a diphthong. I would like to propose that we take that concept one step farther—not English or Singlish, but simply *sounds*.

Have you ever tried to spell a sneezing sound? A burp? A Bronx cheer? You might get close. And that's about as close as you'll ever get to spelling a guitar solo, too. Spell a trumpet sound. I dare you. Now you see what we're up against. Just as a playwright might use "atchoo" rather than "sneeze here," so will music arrangers write "git-a-lit-a git git" rather than "rhythm guitar sounds here." And, to be fair, some arrangers do just that: print brief directions under a bunch of notes—"guitar sound throughout." For some, that liberty is wonderful. For many, the lack of guidance is overwhelming and frustrating.

Remember that Syllables are Physical Guidelines

Because most instrumental sounds are written in some form of syllabification, it is important that you take the time to break the syllables down into their physical acts. Read each one of the syllables below out loud, from left to right. Each line is a grouping. After each group of three, there is an X, which symbolizes a sound that I cannot write for you. Think of this as one of those bizarre SAT questions: *What is that sound?*

JEN	JIN	JN	X
JUM	JIM	JM	X
GAT	GET	GIT	X
CHANG	CHING	CHNG	X

You must consider *why the arranger chose these syllables*. There is a method to their madness. Why do some passages get a softer initial consonant like "J as in Jennifer" rather than the hard "G as in gasoline?" Why is the verse backed with "doos" while the chorus is backed with "dohs?" How does a syllable ending with -*t* differ from those ending with -*ng*? Take the time to *sound the syllables out* and you'll be surprised how much insight you gain into the mind of the arranger. The best part of it all? *If you don't like what they have written,* you can change it!

Listen—Your Ear Is King

As you said the syllables, you may have felt a little silly. That's fine. At this stage in your development, you may have forgotten what it is like to learn a "new instrument." Still, remember that the *result* is our goal. Do whatever is necessary to make the right sound. Of course, sing healthfully, but play around with the position of your jaw, lips, tongue, and sometimes microphone to achieve the sound that sounds good to you.

When was the last time you listened to scat singing? Ella Fitzgerald and Mel Torme make it sound easy, don't they? Try creating a scat like Ella's and you'll soon find out how challenging it is. So is the mastery of a cappella syllabification. But as challenging as it is, through trial and error you will discover what sounds natural and what sounds contrived—*just as you can tell good scat singing from bad scat singing.*

Experiment

Another way to say this is *fail fast.* The theory is simple: *try something.* If it doesn't work, try something else. Use the failures to guide your progress as you move forward from awful to bad to okay to good to great to awesome! Much like a musical game of warmer / colder, the only real way to figure out how you sound great is to burn through a bunch of sounds quickly. I have heard many groups try one sound for an entire song or an entire rehearsal before passing judgement on it . . . What about just "looping" a section of the song, changing sounds on each repeat? Take a 4-bar phrase and just sing it to death. Make it a game by passing it from singer to singer like vocal "hot potato," each one singing the phrase with a sound that has not yet been heard. Steer into the uncomfortable and you can hear 25 options in about 10 minutes.

Of course, don't forget that you can always sing what is on the page. Let's be honest: sometimes "na na na" or "jo-do jo-do" sound just fine. If that's the case, leave it alone. If not, *experiment.*

Additional Tips

Long Notes

Consider how to make a whole note evolve. We know the tried-and-true crescendo and decrescendo. In traditional choral singing, we might even brighten the tone as we travel through the note. For a cappella, try adding an effect to long notes. For instance, "wah" could become a really long "wow" with a slow-motion trip-thong over 4 counts. "Ooh" could go from "ooh" into a grinding "urrr" and then back out to "ooh." This would be like a flange or wah-pedal on a guitar.

Use the Schwa

A *schwa* is a neutral sound, like the sound in the second syllable of the word "sofa." Passages in a cappella music can sometimes sound awkward when sung with vowels that are too pure. For instance, let's take a string of syllables, such as "ba-ba-doo-bop." If sung as written, the distance traveled between AH and OOH requires a lot of effort for a very square-sounding result. Try it by singing the syllables on one pitch on eighth notes at various speeds. See what I mean? Now try it again by replacing the OOH vowel with a schwa (the OOH is the "odd vowel out" so to speak): "ba-ba-də-bop." It becomes much easier to sing, and creates an implied pulse that is more natural. By using the schwa on selected syllables that feel awkward, or by taking every vowel in a passage and "infecting it with the schwa virus," you can achieve more natural flow. For block chords, pure vowels are fantastic. For rhythmic passages, a more neutral vowel set can really keep things flowing naturally.

Addition by Subtraction

A great way to make your songs more interesting is to look for opportunities to change texture. Good arrangements do that for you, but sometimes you just need a little something extra. Consider enhancing your performance by finding a place to subtract something. For instance, if there's a short passage of great-sounding homophonic chords, cut the vocal percussion underneath them. If you have an amazing soloist, consider doing a verse without any backing vocals (just bass, vocal percussion, and the soloist). Sometimes even cutting a climactic whole note one beat short to insert dramatic silence before the chorus kicks in can be effective. You don't have to have everyone sing all the time, even if the arrangement says so. When you alter the texture by subtracting elements, you bring extra attention to what *is happening*. You are saying, "Check this part out—it's so cool!"

What About the Bass and Drums?

The rhythm section is the backbone of any good band. In fact, they are so important, they'll each get their own chapter. For now, let's circle back and summarize our plan of attack to sound authentic.

Summary

 » Listen to the original.

 » Know your form.

 » Work out your syllables.

CHAPTER 7

PRACTICE VS. REHEARSAL

> **"**People do what you inspect,
> not what you expect.**"**
>
> —Lou Gerstner
> Retired CEO of RJR Nabisco and IBM

At this point, we have discussed your rehearsal—how to structure it, how to run it, and musical devices you can use to improve it. What we haven't covered is what happens between rehearsals. It's called practice. Many people think that the time a group spends together is practice. That's because sports teams practice. Individual work for athletes is called conditioning. The terms used by musicians are rehearsal (the entire group working together) and practice (what an individual singer does on their own).

Students should be expected to practice. It's the only way to have a great group. Imagine a football team that only practiced together after school, with none of the players doing any conditioning, weight training, studying the playbook at home, watching other football games, or considering their diet. How good do you think that football team would be?

Similarly, your singers have to condition themselves to be great musicians. They have to tackle many things on their own, including:

» Vocal technique

» Score study

» Polishing the plan

» Vocal health

Vocal Technique—Lessons Are Your Friend

One way to really improve your group is to improve the singers in the group. Of course, you teach technique in your rehearsal, but there's no replacement for one-on-one study. Private lessons that focus on classical technique will improve range, flexibility, tone, and general awareness, all of which can be used by your singers to work through their repertoire on their own to great effect.

Remember, great singing is great singing. Many young singers think that pop and classical singing are as far apart as the colors red and green. In reality, it's more accurate to say that all good singing comes in shades of red. Stylistic concerns may shade the singing, but the technique underneath it all remains the same. Listen to great singers like Whitney Houston, Celine Dion, Ella Fitzgerald, Josh Groban, Michael Bublé, Frank Sinatra, and even Elvis. There's an underlying technique. Kristin Chenoweth is a Broadway phenomenon, but she started out singing gospel and studying opera. If you take the time to listen, you can even hear Madonna's singing improve over time. Lessons help.

Score Study—Learn Your Notes (And More)

There's really nothing more helpful than when students learn their notes *outside* of rehearsal. In addition to notes, there's articulation, dynamics, phrasing, and more. How can you help your singers help you by learning their own parts?

Learning Tracks

Some arrangements come with learning tracks as a practice tool. Learning tracks come with either studio singers or midi (computer generated tones), with the intended part played louder than the others. These are not replacements for music literacy, but they can help your singers get ready for rehearsal. After all, learning tracks can be played in the car, on a dog walk, while exercising, etc.

Recorders

As mentioned in another chapter, digital recorders can help singers immensely. Many students now have this capability on their smartphones as well. If you have to plunk notes in rehearsal, at least have your singers make a recording while you do it. Then they can practice for next time.

Polishing the Plan

In addition to learning notes outside rehearsal, students must take up the task of retaining all articulations, phrasing, and dynamics that were covered in rehearsal. Make sure each student marks their own scores to study at home. I suggest you have all singers mark down everything you say. While you might be making a suggestion for the tenors, the same point may also be helpful to the sopranos. This raises the group's awareness and allows the students to help each other. When they have a sectional or rehearse without you, they can say, "Remember when Mr. McDonald told you to . . ." rather than, "I think you should . . ." It keeps students from getting sensitive to internal coaching.

A good way to tell if students are polishing the plan is to give them a score "quiz." After several rehearsals, give the singers fresh, unmarked music for a song. Maybe even cover up the markings provided by the arranger. Have them go through and mark as many articulations, breath marks, and dynamics as they can remember.

Vocal Health

It is important that your singers consider themselves vocal athletes. Their whole lifestyle contributes to their singing. Therefore, they should develop good habits of vocal health now, which include:

» Stay hydrated. "Pee white, sing right"—Okay, that's a little off-color (pardon the pun), but it holds true. Make sure your singers are drinking plenty of water and other non-caffeinated fluids. Many young people seem to live at Starbucks and thrive on energy drinks. Make sure they know the value of water.

» Avoid overuse/abuse of the voice. Many students talk too much. *Way* too much. They need to remember to avoid screaming (at sporting events, for example) and improper singing. Many young singers use too much "muscle" as they sing to compensate for a lack of technique. They also tend to sing out of their range for fun, another habit to break.

» Get some sleep. The demands on students seems higher than ever, but recent studies show that teens need more sleep than just about anyone. Help them to develop good planning skills so they can keep up with all their responsibilities at home and school. In addition, singers must consider themselves "in training." They have to sleep! This becomes even more important as a big concert approaches. When we need sleep the most, it seems the hardest to get.

» Avoid under-supported singing and unnecessary "marking." Many young singers have the wrong idea of what it means to "mark" their singing. Marking means to sing "half-voice" when one's voice is tired. Unfortunately, many young singers will use this as an excuse to sing poorly. They "mark" when they shouldn't, even doing so when not curbing their habits of talking, shouting, etc. Don't allow marking unless the student has shown they are in need and has taken other steps to stay in good voice. An over-reliance on marking can be a slippery slope.

Summary

» Students should be responsible to retain rehearsal goals and learn their own notes through individual practice.

» Technology such as learning tracks and recorders can help immensely.

» Singers are vocal athletes, and they must go into "training" to maintain good habits:

- Vocal Technique

- Score Study

- Polishing the Plan

- Vocal Health

Refining

CHAPTER 8

THE BALANCING ACT

One of the biggest downfalls of the beginning a cappella group is failing to understand the balance of parts within a performance. I think most singers have a basic knowledge that they can't sing every note the same way. Still, many high school singers are limited to a concert choir experience. They probably have made it as far as "solo vs. choir" or "moving parts sing louder." These are good concepts. Combined with dynamics, they are a solid start. However, a cappella music has more opportunities for changing musical roles than any other genre. Where else might you be a soloist for a full verse, then switch to "playing electric guitar," then switch to singing an internal harmony in homophonic chords? You might even stop singing and become an auxillary vocal percussionist for part of a song.

Singing in an a cappella group is a different experience with every arrangement because each one brings new textures and "instrumentation." Some songs have horn lines and some don't. They may be "rock band," "jazz combo," and everything in between. This means each song is like a new puzzle and good singers find that fascinating. The process is similar to building a piece of furniture with every person in your group owning one tool. You have to plan, communicate, and sometimes trade tools in order to get the job done. Let's start by getting a common vocabulary. Then we'll look at a graph that can help organize your singers and develop their a cappella instincts.

The components of acappella singing include:

» Solo(s)

» Background Vocals

  • Harmonies

  • Echoes/Inserts

- Syllables
- White Notes
» The Rhythm Section
  - Bass
  - Vocal Percussion

Solo

The solo is the melody of the song. The soloist is the "front man" for the group. Remember, you are presenting like a band, so your soloist shouldn't just be louder. They have to be more present in every way: visually, musically, and stylistically.

Background Vocals

Background vocals cover everything that isn't the soloist or rhythm section (bass and drums). Background vocals come in a variety of styles. Depending on how many singers you have and the arrangement, you may have all of these happening at once.

Harmonies

I'm not referring to harmony in the general sense, but to any voices that are directly harmonizing with the soloist. What we consider traditional harmonies might be presented as *syllables* or *white notes*.

Echoes/Inserts

These are bits of singing that accent the soloist's performance. After a soloist's line is finished, *echoes* are used as direct reiterations of the melody or a quick burst of harmony to fill the break until the solo comes back in. Think of the song "Hotel California," where the backup singers echo the lead: "Such a lovely place, (such a lovely place,) such a lovely face." Another example of an insert happens in "Get Ready" by the Temptations. After the soloist sings, the backup singers insert a phrase for emphasis. While the lyric can be the same or different, the *echo/insert* serves the purpose of continuing motion in the music until the soloist enters again.

Syllables

This refers to the nonsense syllables that create rhythmic energy or mimic instruments. I have also heard them affectionately called *jens and jo-dos*. Remember from Chapter 6 that syllables are guidelines to sound, not hard-and-fast words.

White Notes

They don't actually have to be white! Most times, *white notes* are whole-notes or half-notes, but sometimes they can be quarter-notes or dotted-quarters in a song with a slow tempo. *White notes* refers to notes that are static in pitch, and thus require special attention to ensure they are interesting to hear without covering up other parts. Singers can use general dynamics to provide interest (crescendo, decrescendo, etc.). They can also alter the vowel over the course of the note. For instance, while singing a single pitch on a whole note, they can start on "ooh" and over the course of four beats, slowly morph to an "ah." If well executed, this can be a fantastic effect.

The Rhythm Section

The rhythm section is the backbone of your group. Your bass and vocal percussion must stay linked with each other to create a foundation on which the group can sing. The vocal percussion keeps time, but the bass is in charge of the harmonic rhythm. Keeping these two elements working in synchronicity can be the difference between a good group and a great group. Because they are so important, we have given them their own chapters.

The Pyramid of Priority

Take a look at the following diagram. The bottom of the pyramid is divided by a thick black line. This reminds us that our rhythm section is the foundation on which our group always sits. Above that line is the rest of the group. Two lines show us the inverse relationship between the *need to create interest* and *presence in the mix* (volume relationship). For example, the soloist should always be louder than the background vocals, so they don't get lost in the mix. However, solos are inherently interesting. That is not to say that the soloist can go on autopilot (far from it), but with all other things being equal, the melody will naturally sound more interesting to the audience than, for instance, whole notes.

» When your singers sing *white notes*, they will have to figure out ways for the notes to be interesting, but should not be overly present in the mix. White notes can easily cover up other parts.

» *Syllables* are usually rhythmic propellants (like a rhythm guitar part), and thus should be more present in the mix. Still, these parts can be repetitive and thus need to be sung with intensity to avoid monotony. Also, repeated rhythmic figures will need accents to create interest. Many arrangements do not provide accents within repetitive figures, so you'll have to create your own. For more on this, see *Sing in Circles* in Chapter 5 **Rehearsal Techniques**.

» *Harmonies* and *echoes* should be sung in equal volume to the soloist. These brief musical moments are like cherries on a sundae.

As your singers navigate a new chart, they should make a mental map. As they move from *white notes* to *syllables* to *harmonies* to *echoes* they will have to move up and down in volume, while paying close attention to their stylizations. To test this process, take a song you have learned and have your singers sing all the way through without any changes in volume or style. You'll hear an awkward sound where singers and sections pop out of the mix in non-musical ways. Then sing the chart again applying the principles of the *pyramid of priority*. I think you'll be pleased with the results.

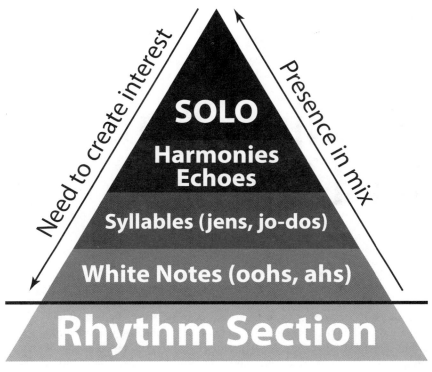

The Pyramid of Priority

Summary

» Each singer must be aware of their role in the arrangement at all times.

» Teach the pyramid of priority to all your singers.

» Map out each song together as a group, noting volume relationships that work within each section of the song.

» Always rehearse with the pyramid of priority in mind.

CHAPTER 9

PLANNING YOUR SET LIST

The main point of your a cappella group is to perform. In fact, it will probably perform more often than any other group you have, because it is most likely smaller and thus more portable than other groups in your program. On top of that, it is singing music that is more accessible to the public at large. "Gigging" is what it's all about.

Therefore, it is important to construct your repertoire into a cohesive *set list*, an order that is your traditional "go-to" gig plan. You can change it at any time to adapt to circumstance, but it should become your go-to song order.

There are several factors that can help in determining your set list:

» Song tempo

» Soloist

» Key of song

» Song style

» Vocal percussion

The goal is to create a set list that has flow—one that takes the audience on a journey. The quickest way to visualize this flow is to picture an hourglass. Trace it from the top down. It starts at the top at its widest point, then narrows gradually to the middle, then expands again to the bottom. Your set list should do the same. It should start with immense energy and presence, then transition to a slower, more subdued pace. After that, it should ramp up to a big finish.

As an example for this chapter, we'll look at a seven-song set. This will afford you somewhere between 20-30 minutes of performance, depending on song length, applause, and talking to the audience (more on that later). The three anchor points of your set are your opener, closer, and ballad. Select those first. After that, you'll want to choose a second song and penultimate song. We'll call the remaining two songs "filler" for lack of a better word. Your seven-song set should look like this:

1. Opener
2. Second Song
3. Filler
4. Ballad
5. Filler
6. Penultimate Song
7. Closer

Opener

Your opener should be a high-energy song with a great soloist. Even better is the opportunity for the solo line to be passed around the group. Because this song is the audience's introduction to your singers, having more solo lines becomes a teaser of things to come. Your opener should be your second-best song, leaving the best song for the closer.

Second Song

The second song is a chance for the energy to relax a little, but don't let the audience off the hook. It's a good idea to get them engaged by immediately going into the second song. Don't allow a dead silence to fall after the applause. You can help this by creating a vamp at the start of your second song, perhaps the bass line and drums from the intro looped over and over. Then one of your more dynamic singers can talk over the vamp, greeting the audience and/or introducing the group if you wish.

Filler #1

Filler is, well . . . filler. I mean, let's be honest. It's hard to have every song have equal impact. Some songs are just "nice songs." While we hope that every song you pick is strong, inevitably some are just going to be not as strong. Filler before the ballad should be the slower of the two filler songs, as the faster filler should help pick up the pace coming out of the ballad.

Ballad

The ballad is in the middle of the set on purpose. It gives the audience an opportunity to sit back and regroup, and gives your singers a chance to breathe (standing still or perhaps sitting on stools). If they are performing properly, they'll need some bodily rest before powering through to the end.

Filler #2

This filler song should be noticeably quicker than the ballad, helping to rev things up towards the end of the set.

Penultimate Song

Penultimate is just a fancy way of saying "next-to-last," and that's what this song is. It should build the energy up for the closer. This is the "set" of the volleyball before the "spike" of the closer.

Closer

This should be your best song. It should blow the doors off. This is the place where you tell the audience to stand and dance along, clap along, or even sing along. Make sure you announce that it is your last song, because then the audience will be more likely to get into it.

Shorter and Longer Sets

The theory is the same, no matter what size the set. We will take our cue from the seven-song set to build other sets.

Three-Song Short Set

1. Opener
2. Second Song or Ballad
3. Closer

Five-Song Medium Set

1. Opener
2. Second Song
3. Ballad
4. Penultimate Song
5. Closer

Longer Sets

If a seven-song set is an hourglass, longer sets look more like a snake that has eaten several rats. You just insert another "bubble" in the middle of your hourglass to stretch your set.

1. Opener
2. Second Song
3. Filler
4. Ballad
5. Fast Filler (second opener style)
6. Filler
7. Ballad
8. Filler
9. Penultimate Song
10. Closer

Additional Guidelines

» Make sure you don't program back-to-back songs in the same key.

» Vary the male and female solos for variety.

» Place newer songs that are being performed for the first time in the middle of the set. Always open and close with confidence.

» Communicate with your vocal percussionist—some songs have patterns that really wear them out. If that's the case, a quick song swap can help them immensely.

» Don't forget the venue. If you're singing for a church event or a retirement home, you'll want to alter your set to include more songs that are appropriate for that audience. Similarly, if you're in the middle school doing a recruiting concert, you might alter the set in the opposite direction.

How to Plan the Set

Make some index cards with the song title, key signature, soloist, tempo, etc. on them. That way, you can switch songs around easily until you find your order. If you keep the cards for every song in your repertoire, then whenever you have to make a different set, you can bring them out again.

When to Talk and What to Say

It's important that you have a rapport with your audience. Singing any amount of songs back-to-back-to-back without the acknowledgement that there are real people in the audience is going to dampen enthusiasm. For most gigs you should have a few talking points in your show. There are no rules on what to say, but here are some ideas:

» Welcome and/or introductions

» Merchandise or future show plugs

» Song trivia

» Thank you

Welcome and/or Introductions

It's the start of the show and before things get rolling, it's time for some of the clichés: "It's great to be here," "We're so excited to sing for you tonight" and "Let me take a moment to introduce the group." Because you don't want the energy to die at the start of a show, it's a good idea to make this quick and possibly do it over a musical vamp.

Merchandise or Future Show Plugs

These can come at any point in the show. If you have CDs or t-shirts to sell, you might as well mention them. The audience won't mind. Be charming. As a school group, we often say, "A lot of school groups try to sell you cheese and sausage, but we've got something way better than that—CDs are on sale in the lobby after the show. All proceeds benefit the choir program." You can also mention your website, future shows, or any music you have available on iTunes.

Song Trivia

One of my pet peeves is when people introduce a song like this: "Our next song is 'Get Ready' by the Temptations." It engages the audience a lot more to say, "Our next song was originally a hit for the Temptations, but was recently redone by Danny Gokey on *American Idol*." Now the audience has a moment to think, "What song is that? I hope it's . . ." There might even be some fun moments where audience members make their guesses with each other.

I tell my kids to never just say the song title. Even something as simple as "This next song was the first single from the new Sarah Bareilles album" feels better than "The next song we are going to sing is 'King of Anything' by Sarah Bareilles."

Another angle on this is to announce more than one song at once: "Our next two songs have something in common. They were both #1 singles in their time, and have appeared on movie soundtracks. The first topped the charts in 1985 and the second in 2005."

Thank You

Gratitude is important. Hopefully, your group is performing at a number of venues and each one has different people to thank. They could include:

- » Choir boosters
- » Whomever hired you ("We'd like to thank Larry Smith and the Rotary Club for inviting us here tonight")
- » Director
- » Sound technician
- » Other groups on the program
- » Audience (for being so great)

Thank yous are great right before the last song. The singers get one last chance to breathe before laying out their high-energy finish, and you can also let people know this is the last song (subliminal message: let's crank up the energy, then please give us a standing ovation).

What to Do Before the Show

You'll need at least two copies of your set list for your performance. One should be on stage for the singers to reference. Make sure the paper is large enough to be easily seen and use a Sharpie® or other fat marker to write the titles in large, clear lettering. It could be helpful to write the key of each song next to the title so the pitch-blower has a reference.

Another copy of your set list is for your sound board operator. They will need the list to contain not only the titles, but also a listing of who has each solo. If the board operator is not familiar with your group, you can help them immensely by indicating the microphone channel number that will be used. Also include an indication for when there will be bits of talking. Don't forget to talk through the set with them before the show for best results.

Summary

As you plan your performance, consider all the factors of your time on stage:

» Length of the show (factor for applause)

» Song flow (tempi, keys, soloists)

» When and how to talk

» A clearly printed set list for the stage and sound board operator

CHAPTER 10

YOUR VISUAL PLAN

Like any other performance, there is a visual component to a cappella. You'll find a whole range of styles out there, from general "winging it" all the way to full-blown choreography. There is no right way to craft your visual plan, but I do suggest you craft it. Even "winging it" requires some guidelines.

You know more about visual performance than you think, even if you have no background in dance or show choir. We can all recognize things that look awkward and things that look good. It is important that you trust your gut and give visual coaching a try, even if it isn't your strength.

Your biggest asset in visual coaching is your musicianship. Visual presentation should enhance the musical presentation at all times. Using the guidelines below will help you uncover the visual plan already hidden inside your music.

Establish a Common Vocabulary

It is critical that your students share a common understanding of terms. The most common are:

» *Stage Left*: Area to the left of a performer (when facing the audience)

» *Center Stage*: "Middle" area of the stage

» *Stage Right*: Area to the right of a performer (when facing the audience)

» *Downstage*: "Front" of the stage (closest to the audience)

» *Upstage*: "Back" of the stage (furthest from the audience)

» *Outside*: The area away from center stage (for instance, a singer's *outside* arm is their left arm if they are stage left)

» *Inside*: The area towards center stage (for instance, a singer's *inside* arm is their right arm if they are stage left)

» *Reference Position*: The "default" position, in which all singers are slightly angled toward center, as if making a subtle rainbow. This allows the singers to see the audience and still see each other.

» *Down the Tiles*: An alternate position in which you face out so that your shoulders are parallel to the back wall. You are completely facing the audience straight-on with no curve. A straight line of singers across the front of the stage would be considered facing "Down the Tiles."

Movement Should Reflect the Music

In order for your performance to have maximum impact, all movement should reflect the music. It's almost like telling the audience what they are hearing. The audience likes this, possibly because it confirms that everything they are hearing is on purpose. Audiences like confident singers more than perfection, although we strive to provide them with both. The best compliment you can get is, "We loved watching you sing."

Here are some suggestions to help you map a visual plan for each song. Take the time to write your plan down, even making notes in your music for reference. All planned moves should be rehearsed by the singers as often as they can while they are singing. Practice makes permanent.

The Capsule Concept (also mentioned in Chapter 14 The Solo Vocalist)

The *capsule concept* refers to the underlying message of a given song. In order for every member of the group to project a uniform visual image, they must all support the *capsule concept*. When considering the *capsule concept*, start by trying to complete this sentence: "This song is about _____." Then try to take the song and distill it down to one emotional keyword. By doing this, you can become truly unified as a group.

Perhaps your one-sentence summary is: "This song is about a man who lost his girlfriend to another man." Some of the singers might assume the emotional keyword is *sad*. Still others might think *regret*. Others might think *jealousy*. Maybe someone even thinks *rage*. There is a difference between *sad* and *regret,* just as there is a difference between *happiness* and *anticipation*. This might seem like an exercise in subtlety, but the *capsule concept* will influence every decision in a song. It will most directly affect your visual plan, because the cornerstone of every performance is what is projected on your faces.

Make a Picture of Each Section of the Song

Imagine that you are taking snapshots of your performance, one for each section of each song. When you finish the concert and print the pictures, you should be able to go back and assemble the concert from start to finish based on your stage configuration, soloist, and body presence. You took the time to map out each song's sections for musical reasons. Now take the time to establish the "snapshot" on stage for each section so that your singers always have a "home base" to reference as they perform. You can use the other tools in this chapter to decide what each snapshot should be.

Proximity

This refers to where your singers are placed on stage. You could make a formation if you like, but you should be primarily concerned with where the singers are located in both the X and Y axes that define stage left vs. right and upstage vs. downstage, respectively. Remember:

» Louder, faster sections lend themselves to spreading out and coming downstage toward the audience

» Softer, more intimate passages lend themselves to a tighter position that is located more center stage and/or upstage

» Singers who are linked with similar instruments should often stand together. You might have a "horn line" of singers together in one area, rhythm section (bass and drums) in another, and the soloist up front. When the "instrumentation" changes, your position can change, too.

Visual Focus

By using your body angles, you can direct the audience's focus to different areas of the stage. Oftentimes, you would direct them to look at the soloist by having the background singers do the same. If the song is a poignant ballad, I suggest giving the soloist some separation from the group and having all backup singers focused on the soloist. In faster songs, the background singers can move and groove, but they should still have a general awareness of where the soloist is and face towards him/her as a group. Even if a group of backup vocalists are having interplay with each other (which is good), their group should focus on the soloist. Sometimes you might want to draw attention to a musical effect that  occurs when the soloist is resting, such as a drum fill or a horn line. In that case the soloist should change their posture and join the group in deferring to those with the featured line. In a homophonic section, de-emphasize the soloist by having everyone stand together, facing the audience.

Where Are You Looking?

The eyes say it all. When a singer looks at the audience, they invite the listeners into the performance. What does it say when a singer looks at the stage? What if they close their eyes? Who gets invited along then? I suggest a simple rule: your

singers can look at each other to have a fun "jam moment," they can look at the soloist, or they can look at the audience. They should not look anywhere else except when intentionally planned for effect. Your singers should also avoid looking around too often, jumping from one focus point to the next every other measure. Stick with a focus point for at least a full phrase, maybe two or more before finding a new focus.

Moving to the Beat

It is common for singers to move to the beat, "jamming" along in their own little world. However, if every singer moves differently it can erode timekeeping as well as provide a disjointed visual presentation. Moving to the beat should be planned—not *how*, but *when*. Remember our discussion on *singing in circles*? Each singers' movements should fit into the pulse of the song, be it a driving uptune, a half-time groove, or a ballad. Many ballads require little-to-no movement at all. But don't forget that planning a complete freeze of motion during an uptune or one small section of movement during a ballad can provide a visual climax.

Accent Moves

Your song will have accents, echoes, group rests, and other places of brief unity within an otherwise complex texture. A brief hand gesture, body angle change, or movement freeze on such accents can provide extra pop to your performance.

Use Your Levels

In addition to changing body angles, you can sometimes change body levels. Unlike concert choir, you can:

» Go down on one knee

» Go down on both knees

» Crouch low to the ground

» Put one foot up on a stool or monitor

» Jump up in the air

» "Lay back" so that your weight sinks into your hips, making you slightly shorter

» Bend at the waist, then rise back to standing over a certain number of counts

These level changes ought not be done just to do them, but they can really bring out powerful moments in the music. They can also reflect dynamic changes for your group, and can really provide interest if the soloist exploits them. Music that is too similar for too long can create boredom, and so can lack of levels. Now you have X, Y, and Z axes to handle.

In the event that you're on a stage with some form of risers, you can get on and off the risers in various configurations to change levels. Likewise, you can use stools to create positions for seated singing (often done for ballads).

What Do I Do With My Arms?

If each person in the group has a microphone, you use one arm to hold that microphone. As you make your visual plan, don't forget that when staging a move or position,

the mic hand counts. Always match inside or outside hand. If your singers angle towards center stage, using the inside hand as your mic hand will keep your body open to the audience. If the group opens up away from center, the opposite is true.

If you are imitating an instrument, you can use your hands to mimic playing that instrument. It sounds a little hokey, but it works.

If you are holding nothing and are not imitating an instrument, remember that:

» Most singers tend to keep their elbows too close to their body, minimizing their presence on stage.

» Any arm movements must be sharp, with definite starting and ending points on specific beats.

» Keep presence in your arms (and body) at all times.

» When freestyling, parallel gestures (both arms looking the same, as if mirroring) are weaker than asymmetrical gestures. However, parallel gestures can look great for choreographed moves.

Additional Tips

Stay in the light. If you are on a stage with lights, find the place where the light stops. Do not leave the light. If you can't feel light on your face, you're out of the light, and people will have a tough time seeing you. (If you use wireless microphones, sometimes you can go out in the audience and still remain in the light.)

When rehearsing, ask the singers to try some moves of their own. You'll often find one student who comes up with great stuff the others can copy. Similarly, you might find that many students have certain movement patterns in common. Finding what the singers instinctively do, then enhancing that (rather than creating arbitrary choreography) will keep them looking natural on stage. It will also help them remember the plan.

Commit to every move you make. Watch out for weak body presence. Even standing still requires a plan, effort, and better posture than normal.

Visual Rehearsal Tips

Now that you have some tools to begin crafting your visual plan, here are some ways to hone your product.

Video Review

Just like football players watch films, we should watch our performances. Either one song at a time, or sometimes an entire set (for flow, talking, singing, and visual elements), the video review is invaluable. Watch a performance and take notes. Have each singer share with the group one thing that looked great and one thing that needs improvement. Aren't we all our own worst critics?

Another video review tip is *fast-forward*. Start the performance you wish to review, then put the playback on fast-forward. You'll either see the singers moving around the stage, changing positions, and using their arms to create interest or you'll see a bunch of kids who look like they are vibrating in place. If it's boring on fast-forward, it's definitely boring in real time.

Imagineering

Once the plan is in place, there's great value in *imagineering*. This can be done in rehearsal or at home (or both). The goal is to have the entire group close their eyes and picture themselves on stage. Literally blow the pitch so everyone is imagineering in the right key. Tell them that after you count off, they are to silently imagine the entire performance from start to finish. They should see the visual plan happening perfectly. They should hear every sound perfectly in tune. Do the exercise with them. When you are done, announce "stop." How many students were done at the same time? This process allows us to plant the seeds of perfect performance in our minds. If we can see it, if we can believe it—we can achieve it.

Silent Runs

Get on stage. Blow the pitch. Start the song—with no singing. Every singer must "mouth it" as if they are singing along with a track. Every move should be made. They should replicate the performance as if someone is watching it on mute. When the singing is gone, the visual performance is amplified. Immediately following this exercise, make them do it with the same visual intensity, adding the singing. This not only helps your visuals, but timekeeping as well.

Still Shots

With today's digital cameras, this exercise is easier than ever, and it's just what we mentioned at the start of this chapter. Run your song (or set), with the director snapping one or two photos during each section of the performance. Immediately print the photos and present them to the group to put in chronological order.

One Man Out

Every so often, pick a student to sit out in the audience for a performance. Not only will they be able to give some pointers in rehearsal, they might be able to address some issues outside rehearsal in a more casual setting. Students often "think they're doing it" until someone other than the director says, "I see you trying, but it needs to be much bigger."

Two Crucial Concepts to Remember

Break It All Down and Have Patience

It is important to remember that once your plan is in place, it must be polished until it sparkles. This requires close attention to detail and tons of patience. Ultimately, you'll decide how clean is "clean enough," but remember that everything needs attention. Body posture, foot position, arm angles, head position, eye focus, and spatial relationships on stage are all items that need cleaning. You will need to isolate and examine each move beat by beat to make sure they all match. While this will take a lot of time, remember that as your singers grow more and more accustomed to this level of visual cleanliness, they will soon self-correct. As they grow into aware performers, the time required to clean their moves will be less.

Every Move Needs a Motivation

We have mentioned that every part of your visual plan should be created with the *capsule concept* in mind. In addition, every move must have a purpose that is motivated by that concept. If your singers are merely executing choreography because you said to do it, they will always look stilted and flat. Singers who move with purpose in order to express an emotion will always thrill an audience, even when their execution is not perfect. Remember, "ya gotta have heart!" Audiences do not want to be impressed by perfection. They want to be moved. If they get both, so much the better.

Summary

Every performance must have a visual plan, even if there is no choreography. The plan already lives in the music; you just need to extract it. Make a plan that is intuitive for your singers and write it down. Make sure it comes from the heart, and so you can perform with conviction every time. Practice it, review it, and perfect it!

CHAPTER 11

WHAT TO WEAR?

One of the first things students tend to ask is, "What are we going to wear?" I'm sure you've noticed that high school students are very concerned with appearance. Having a cool outfit for your group is essential to their confidence and sense of identity. In concert choirs and show choirs, outfits are more like costumes. They match to create unity. In a cappella groups, there is a greater focus on individuality, so there is usually more emphasis on clothing "concepts" than on matching outfits. Can you match? Sure. It's your group. There's nothing wrong with matching. However, since that's a familiar concept, we'll explore other ideas to help expand your horizons.

Do You Need More Than One Outfit?

There are many types of gigs, and so having more than one type of outfit can be helpful. If you plan several outfits in advance, you'll never again have to spend time debating during the season. Here are some suggested types of outfits:

Standard/Formal

To be used at all gigs unless otherwise specified. This would be your most coordinated outfit. It could be matching or loosely themed. If using a loose theme, you're basically agreeing to color or clothing families. For instance, you could say, "Wear anything you want as long as it is . . ."

>> Denim and *pick one color*   >> Black and *pick one color*

» Black and *multi-colored*

» Khaki and *multi-colored*

When I say *pick one color*, I mean that everyone in the group should have the same color. For instance, if the group is to be dressed in black and red, there are many variations your students will use to create their own presence on stage. One girl might wear a black dress with a red sash. Another girl might wear red pants and a black top. A boy might wear black pants with a red shirt and black vest. Another boy might wear black pants with a black dress shirt and red t-shirt underneath. You get the picture.

When I say *multi-colored,* I mean that your singers should stay within a color family. Sometimes students don't easily grab onto terms like "primary colors," "earth tones," or "pastels." I have had luck using the Skittles® analogy because they come in different groupings such as original, tropical, mint, etc. Your students should pick colors that coordinate as if they had opened a bag of Skittles and dumped them out on the counter. Original Skittles are primary and secondary colors; a pastel color would look out of place in that grouping. No matter how you explain your color family, it's important that everyone fully grasp the idea before they go shopping. Of course, if you are

providing everyone's outfits, this isn't an issue. I have found that allowing the students to pick their own outfit within guidelines allows for more pride and ownership. As another plus, students coordinating to go shopping together on their own time is a fun, social bonding experience.

Spiritwear

Since you will likely perform at school functions, you may sometimes choose to wear *spiritwear.* Once again, the students can express themselves within a theme, and if they sing at a pep rally or ballgame, they'll be comfortable when the performance is over.

Casual/Travel Outfit

If your group will do any touring or traveling, it isn't a bad idea to have at least one casual outfit. It doesn't take much effort to coordinate, and allows for a good look on field trips or festivals. Some groups will buy matching t-shirts or polo shirts and then wear them with khaki pants or jeans.

Summer Outfit

Once your group is established, the community may have interest in performances for summertime activities, such as Independence Day, Labor Day, or other local events. Summer outfits require some thought to stay cool without becoming overly casual.

No matter what you wear, make sure you always communicate your guidelines for style, color, and condition of the outfits. I once made the mistake of telling my group to show up "dressed nice, like you're going to church." The event was a memorial service for fallen police officers. One of my singers showed up in cargo shorts and flip-flops, looking horribly out of place. He looked at me and said, "This is how I go to church." I had to admit, that's all the guidance I had given.

Summary

» Looking good is important, while matching is not.

» Matching is not forbidden, but it's not required.

» Communicate your plan effectively.

» Have a standard of presentation that looks professional.

» Clothes must be neat, clean, and fit well.

I'm stating the obvious as a reminder to you to state the obvious to your singers. They are still students, after all.

Specializing

Vocal Percussion
by Jake Moulton

Few things define the contemporary a cappella style more than vocal percussion. Unfortunately, this form of music making is foreign to many. As a director, you might not be versed in vocal percussion, but you owe it to yourself (and your group) to become familiar with it, and yes—functional at doing it.

You've probably spent a long time choosing the repertoire for your group. How much did the arrangements cost? Did you create them? Did your group arrange them together? How long did it take? Now, considering your answers, why would you just tell someone to make some "drum sounds" and hope for the best? Please don't underestimate your vocal percussionist's ability to make or break your music. I guarantee that after reading this chapter, you'll not only have the tools to perform vocal percussion and "human rhythm" sounds yourself, but also to teach them and write patterns for your students to follow.

Human Rhythm vs. Vocal Percussion vs. Beatboxing What Is What?

Human Rhythm

The best way to describe Human Rhythm (let's refer to it as HR) is rhythmic patterns created using basic human or guttural sounds. This is the easiest way to add rhythm to your arrangements, as it requires little thought or practice to create each individual sound. You can think of these sounds (and describe them to your students) as primal expressions of emotion and rhythm, and in the right setting they can perfectly compliment and drive a song without being overpowering. These sounds play the role of percussion instruments without focusing on their imitation, keeping your students' focus on keeping time and groove rather than whether or not they're making the "right" sound. Speaking of imitation . . .

Vocal Percussion

Vocal Percussion (or VP as we'll refer to it) is much easier to wrap your head around than Human Rhythm, even though the execution doesn't come *quite* as naturally. Simply put, it's the imitation or approximation of percussion instruments. Even though there are countless percussion instruments to choose from, it's fairly safe to assume that, for the most part, your students will be using six basic percussion sounds. With this palette of sounds (and with the occasional supplemental HR sounds), you should be able to successfully perform most songs and styles comfortably *and* musically. The basic vocal percussion sounds that you'll be using are bass (or kick) drum, rim shot, snare drum, hi-hat, tom-toms, and cymbals. When you and your students have a good understanding of both HR and VP, you can consider moving on to the next step . . . beatboxing.

Beatboxing

What is beatboxing? Good question. I'll let you know when I figure it out. I've had a long, tumultuous relationship with the word beatboxing (BB for short). When I made the leap from novice to intermediate, I decided and professed that I was a beatboxer, citing my desire to respect the art's origin (i.e. the "streets") as my reasoning. It wasn't until a couple years ago that I truly realized the difference between VP and BB, what the role of each was, and where I fit in.

Beatboxing is a form of vocal percussion, absolutely, but so much more. My favorite definition comes from one of the many elementary school children to whom I've had the pleasure of teaching this art form. She described it as "music with your mouth" and was spot on. Beatboxing is making and *being* the music, not just rhythm. Don't get me wrong. Often times, beatboxers may choose to just make rhythmic sounds, especially when working with other musicians; however, even in those instances, their choices of sounds vary.

Please let me generalize for a moment. Most beatboxers tend to focus on imitating or creating more synthesized percussion sounds rather than necessarily focusing on the imitation of real percussion instruments. Also, many will steer clear of using crash cymbals and tom-toms. The palette for beatboxers is truly limitless if they want it to be, but often times, most rely on three basic percussion sounds for their fundamental beat: bass drum, electronic sounding rim shot, and hi-hat. Once the beat has been established, *then* the magic can happen.

As I mentioned, beatboxing is music with your mouth. That means that many beatboxers not only play the role of the drummer or percussionist, but a member of the band, DJ, or even singer . . . all at the same time.

Which Is Appropriate for You?

Though you should absolutely encourage your students to investigate beatboxing by challenging themselves to add to their palette of percussive sounds and learn more about their voices through experimentation with instrument mimicry, you'll find that using HR and VP will be more appropriate as accompaniment. Accordingly, those two techniques will be the focus of this chapter. Remember, the group, music, and audience come first. There will be an appropriate time for your beatboxer to shine! But, we'll talk about solos later.

And speaking of appropriate . . . should there always *be* a drum part?

Now that all of your hard work in forming an a cappella group has paid off, what kind of role do you give to your vocal percussionist? This part can be a challenge. As the leader of your group, you need to know when to let your vocal percussionist do what he/she thinks is appropriate and when to write out the percussion part. Sometimes you might use a combination of both, and sometimes you might not utilize vocal percussion at all. As strange as this analogy may be, contextually, vocal percussionists are like nuclear weapons—just because you have them doesn't mean you should use them.

Your use of VP should always be intentional. It will depend on what you deem necessary to get the sound you want for your arrangement, as well as the skill level and musicianship of your chosen vocal percussionist. If you've chosen to use VP on a song, and your student is new to vocal percussion, it may be best to

VP Tip #1

Be true to the music— not every song needs VP.

have them focus on HR and slowly work them into imitating the drums. However, if they have some experience with VP, you might give them more, according to what is going to sound best for the song.

If you've chosen not to use a vocal percussionist for a particular arrangement, it's perfectly acceptable to have them sing their respective part. However, if they're NOT a vocalist, I'd recommend having them either leave the stage or step aside, rather than sing a part they're not comfortable with or lip-syncing. If nothing else, it will add to the show by offering both visual AND aural variety. It's like killing two birds with one vocal percussionist.

VP Tip #2

If you're not using a vocal percussionist, and they're not a vocalist, consider having them leave the stage or step aside from the group.

Now that you've decided what song to do and chosen whether you want to use HR, VP, or nothing at all, it's time to figure out the sounds. Assuming that I don't need to teach you the sound of silence (indulgent Simon & Garfunkel reference), I'll begin with Human Rhythm.

Human Rhythm

As mentioned earlier, Human Rhythm is basically the use of guttural sounds to represent percussion instruments. This is not only a simple solution for adding rhythm to a song for those who are still learning VP, but also adds a raw, human element that vocal percussion doesn't offer. I love what both styles have to offer separately, but the combination is where the magic truly happens. But, we're getting ahead of ourselves!

A musical beat is typically outlined by the bass and snare drums, and these are the focus of Human Rhythm, along with the use of breath and the occasional vocal percussion rim shot or hi-hat.

The HR Bass Drum

This is about as easy as it gets. In your lower vocal register, lightly say the word "uh."

🔊 Example #1: Human Rhythm Bass Drum *

Ok, now try it again. This time make the pitch a little lower and the note more staccato. Perfect. I can almost hear you from here . . . and from the past when I wrote this. **Note:** higher voices, please relax. As much as this sound requires a lower voice, it's also the *only* Human Rhythm or Vocal Percussion sound that does. Let me remind you that HR is more about feel and attitude than about how low your voice is.

🔊 Example #2: Human Rhythm Bass Drum For Higher Voices

Back to work. Take a minute and experiment with different open vowel sounds in your lower register. Perhaps try: uh, eh, oh, and ee.

🔊 Example #3: Human Rhythm Bass Drum Alternate Vowels

This is extremely important: figure out what works for you! We're all built differently.

The HR Snare Drum

Here's another sound that should come quite naturally: "ah." However, the "pitch" will be significantly higher. I put the word pitch in quotation marks because you aren't actually singing the word. The pitch and timbre of the sound are created by the shape you're making with your mouth and the speed of the air coming out of it.

Have you ever eaten too much garlic and then had to go out in public? You know that thing we do to check our breath? It's like that. Go ahead and try it—cup your hand in front of your face and say "hah" or "hoh." Mint? Seriously though, perhaps you understand now how pitch and timbre can be affected by mouth shape and air speed.

🔊 Example #4: Breath Check

🔊 Example #5: Hahs and Hohs

Now that we all know what your breath smells like and you've minted up, let's try the HR Snare. Instead of the breath check "hah" or "hoh," try removing the "h" at the beginning. This should leave you with a sharp, glottal attack at the beginning of your sound.

🔊 Example #6: Glottal Ah and Oh

🔊 Example #7: HR Snare

The Breathing Hi-Hat

Congratulations! You have what you need to keep the beat. The next step is something that you've already proven to be great at: *breathing*. The only difference

Visit alfred.com/acappellapop to listen to the audio samples.

is that we're going to utilize your breath as rhythm. Take a deep breath, listening to the pitch of your breath. Exhale. Now, inhale quickly and exhale just as fast. Do you hear the difference? If not, keep trying. Experiment with inhalation and exhalation at different speeds and with different mouth shapes and vowel sounds (ah, oh, oo, huh) to figure out what is most comfortable and sounds the best.

🔊 Example #8: HR Long and Short Breaths, Inward and Outward

🔊 Example #9: HR Breath Vowels, Inward and Outward

Keep in mind that as much as your vowel choice affects the sound, so does your mouth shape and the amount of space you create in your mouth. One of my favorite breathing sounds is created using a big, cheesy grin. Smile, resting your top teeth on your bottom teeth and quickly breathe in. Sounds cool, doesn't it? This is a slightly affected breath sound, similar to the open breathing hi-hat you'll soon learn about in the Vocal Percussion section.

🔊 Example #10: HR Smiling Breath, Inward and Outward

HR Notation and Practice Patterns

Now that you've learned the basic sounds, it's time to put them together and write them out for your students to learn. The HR Bass and Snare Drums are pretty simple. I write them using the syllables desired for performance. For example, in 4/4 time with a bass drum on beats 1 and 3 and a snare on beats 2 and 4, it would look like this:

UH AH UH AH

Notice that instead of note heads, I've used slashes with stems to depict the rhythm and placed the desired syllables underneath each respective note. Try the pattern slowly. Though this pattern is simple, *please* don't practice it too fast!

Now that you've mastered your first HR pattern, it's time to add breath! Breath notation will be a little different. Underneath each HR breath syllable we will use a left or right facing arrow. An arrow pointing left (←) represents an inward breath or sound. Obviously, that leaves the right arrow (→) to represent an outward sound. For the time being, nearly all the sounds you will be learning and notating will be made through exhalation. Thus, I'll only notate outward sounds in reference to HR breathing, as well as more challenging VP breathing and hi-hat patterns. For now, let's try a simple HR pattern that incorporates breathing.

VP Tip #3

Take time to become comfortable with the sounds and patterns at a slow tempo before speeding up!

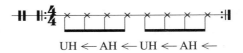

UH ← AH ← UH ← AH ←

Notice that this pattern is broken down into eighth notes with breaths being taken on the second half of every beat. This is where your HR groove should really begin making sense. Take a moment to experiment with the velocity and duration of each sound. Also, note that each of the breaths are inward. If you feel that you're taking in too much air, occasionally replace an inward breath with a similarly pitched and shaped outward breath.

Vocal Percussion Gateway Sounds

Now that you've learned how to perform, explain, and notate HR, it's time to venture into the magical world of VP. Now, rather than throwing your students into imitating a drum set, it's best to transition them slowly. How? Through gateway sounds.

Gateway sounds are simply basic vocal percussion sounds that easily slip into an HR groove, allowing your budding vocal percussionist to practice new sounds while maintaining the groove style (HR) to which they are accustomed. Moreover, these three sounds bring a new amazing depth to Human Rhythm. In fact, I'll bet that once your students add these sounds to their palette, they'll never go back.

The Hi-Hat Cymbal

A hi-hat cymbal is actually just two cymbals that have been mounted together on a special stand. The cymbals face each other and can be moved together and apart through the use of a foot pedal. The hi-hat provides much of the activity in a drum-beat, often being played on every eighth note. In order to vary the sound of the hi-hat, it can be played closed, open, or alternating between the two.

The Vocal Percussion Hi-Hat

Just as the hi-hat is a fundamental part of a drum set, it's also one of the basic building blocks of vocal percussion and beatboxing. Strangely, it is also one of the easiest sounds to create. Though there are different types of hi-hats, they all have the same base: the letter "t."

Let me clarify. Typically, people will automatically say "tea" or "tuh" when you tell them to use the sound of the letter "t." When you tell your students how to make this sound, explain that the hi-hat is made using the SOUND of the letter "t," not the word. For example, try saying the word "tool." When you remove the sound "ool" you're left with just the sound of the letter "t" and the sound of a closed vocal percussion hi-hat.

🔊 Example #11: Basic VP Closed Hi-Hat

Now that you understand how the basic sound is made, let's take it a step further. I've found that the most realistic hi-hat sound is created by slightly adjusting your "t" sound into a smile. Smile and clench your teeth together, with your top teeth overlapping your bottom teeth while creating the sound of the letter "t"—it will sound much more like an actual hi-hat. I like to call this my "Fancy Hat" as it definitely sounds more realistic. Another way to think of it is this: smile with your teeth clenched and make a hissing sound. Now, if you add a "t" at the beginning and experiment with different lengths of hissing, you'll soon find a hi-hat that works for you.

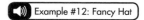

As for notation of the basic hi-hat and the Fancy Hat, both can be written interchangeably at your discretion. They can be notated just as you would imagine, using the letter "t." Also, if you care to notate accents in your hi-hat line, you could simply capitalize the letters.

Let try a simple Basic VP Closed Hi-Hat pattern. When you're ready, try using the Fancy Hat instead. Do you hear the difference? I do.

t t t t t t t t

Note: Simply accenting certain hi-hats will not only bring much more life to your hi-hat pattern, but also to every other pattern you use in the future.

Now try accenting the first eighth note of every beat:

T t T t T t T t

If you're feeling wild, try using sixteenth notes and accenting the first note of every beat:

T t t t T t t t T t t t T t t t

Remember—don't go too fast! Practicing at a slower tempo will help improve your time keeping, as well as the accuracy of your VP sounds.

From now on, it's up to you which hi-hat you choose: the Basic VP Closed Hi-Hat or the Fancy Hat. As they really are interchangeable, there is no need for me to notate them in future practice patterns. Just remember to always experiment with different sounds, pitches, and durations of sound in order to keep your patterns interesting!

Notating the Extension of Sounds

Before moving on, let's quickly address how to notate the sustaining of sound over time. For example, you may want a hi-hat to last two eighth notes or two sixteenth notes. The notation is simple and you'll thank me for it later! The easiest way to notate it to use a simple underscore "_." Try the hi-hat pattern below and when you see the underscore, simply don't make a sound. In the next section, you can try extending an open hi-hat sound when you see the underscore.

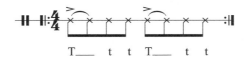

The Vocal Percussion Open Hi-Hat

Now, let's make things a little more interesting. One way to give your hi-hat pattern more feeling is to simply vary the length. By re-adding the "s" that you removed when learning the more realistic sounding hi-hat, you can turn that closed hi-hat sound into an open one. Try making a long "tssss" sound and you'll hear what I mean. Remember to smile, attack the "t" and let the "ssss" quickly diminish from loud to soft to silent.

🔊 Example #13: Open Hi-Hat

Too easy? Then it's time to practice using the open hi-hat in a few simple hi-hat patterns. As you've surely imagined, the open hi-hat can be notated with a simple "tss", which I'll capitalize to demonstrate that the accent should be on it, rather than the regular hi-hat. Also, remember what to do when you see an underscore! When following an open hi-hat pattern, you can assume that you should carry the sound over the next subdivision of the beat. For most other sounds, including the VP Bass Drum, VP Rim Shot, and VP Snare Drum, you should assume that the underscore is silent. (Practice patterns should be read from left to right.)

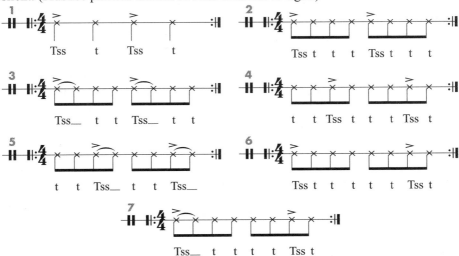

Closing the Hi-Hat

For a more realistic hi-hat closing sound, try adding an "ut" on the next subdivision after the open hi-hat sound. Try to keep the "t" soft, unlike the hi-hat sound. Do this by cutting off the air when your tongue hits your teeth. In fact, it may sound almost like a "d." For example, try this pattern:

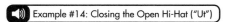

If you don't vocalize, or use your vocal cords when sounding the "ut" sound, you should hear a nice, short completion to the open hi-hat. Try it!

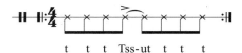

Example #14: Closing the Open Hi-Hat ("Ut")

Also, notice the difference in the feel of the pattern when you simply move your open hi-hat to the right an eighth or sixteenth note. Amazing, isn't it?

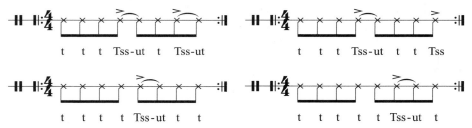

Amazing, right? I thought you'd like that! Now, for the good stuff . . .

The Inward Vocal Percussion Open Hi-Hat

You're learning so much so fast that it's time I reward you. "With what?" you ask? With one of the most valuable sounds you'll learn, the Inward VP Open Hi-Hat. I know, it already sounds complicated; however, it's simple. And with this little sound, you'll be able to keep your beat going as long as you want without taking a break! Trust me, you'll thank me later!

Say the word "the." Do you feel where your tongue sits against your teeth when you prepare to say the word? Perfect. Now, put your tongue in position to say "the" again. This time, try sucking a short burst of air in between your tongue and your teeth. Do you hear that? Sounds pretty real, doesn't it? Not only will this be one of your most useful sounds, it will also be one of your most realistic.

Example #15: Inward VP Open Hi-Hat

If realism is what you're going for, try adding this little trick. At the very end of your inward hi-hat, while breathing *inward*, add the word "thup." This mimics the sound of the hi-hat closing again, but the inward breath makes the sound far more metallic and realistic. Give it a try!

Example #16: Closing the Inward VP Open Hi-Hat

Well done! You've got the hi-hat sound down pat! But, before we can move on to the next sound, you should decide how to notate the Inward Hi-Hat. Just like in HR, the inward sound must be notated a little differently. Underneath the usual open hi-hat notation, simply use the same left arrow you used when notating a breath in HR. It looks like this: T̲ss

Now, let's practice a few hi-hat patterns using what we've learned so far, and combine our newfound hi-hat friend with what we know of HR. At this point, you should have everything you need to successfully provide rhythm for your group.

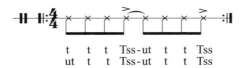

```
t    t    t    Tss-ut    t    t    Tss
ut   t    t    Tss-ut    t    t    Tss
```

On the repeat, the first hi-hat sound becomes the closing of the last open hi-hat.

🔊 Example #17: Hi-Hat Practice Pattern One

This will take some getting used to, especially when we come to the Inward VP Open Hi-Hat.

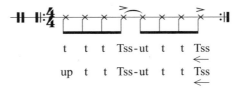

```
t    t    t    Tss-ut    t    t    Tss
                                   ←
up   t    t    Tss-ut    t    t    Tss
                                   ←
```

For this pattern, on the repeat, the first hi-hat *again* becomes the closing of the previous Inward VP Open Hi-Hat, which is the "thup" sound.

🔊 Example #18: Hi-Hat Practice Pattern Two

Now try sixteenth notes.

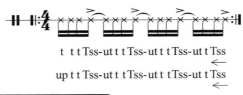

```
t  t t Tss-ut t t Tss-ut t t Tss-ut t Tss
                                      ←
up t t Tss-ut t t Tss-ut t t Tss-ut t Tss
                                      ←
```

🔊 Example #19: Hi-Hat Practice Pattern Three

Practice these patterns for a while until the breathing and repeats become natural.

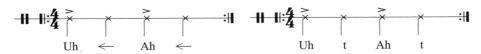

```
Uh   ←    Ah   ←              Uh   t    Ah   t
```

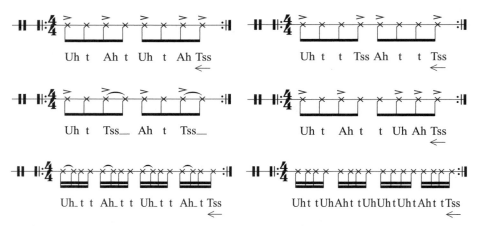

Notice that on these particular patterns, the closing of the hi-hat doesn't work without sacrificing your HR Bass Drum. Thus, you should make the sound normally so as to make the HR Bass Drum sound directly on the downbeat.

The Last of the Gateway Sounds

Congratulations on making it this far without losing your mind. You're almost there! You've made it to the last of the Gateway Sounds: the VP Rim Shot.

A rim shot is the sound made when a drumstick is struck against the rim of the snare drum. To make a lighter sound, only the rim is struck. A heavier rim shot can be made by hitting the snare drum's head and the rim at the same time.

Lucky you, the VP Rim Shot is another simple sound to make, and one that will prove useful for the remainder of your VP or beatboxing career! It is simply made with the sound of the letter "k" and can be notated as such. Now remember, I said the *sound* of the letter "k." For example, say the word "kick." Once again, try saying just the beginning of the word and you have the sound of your VP Rim Shot. Also, remember to *not* vocalize while making this sound. No singing or speaking a pitch! The "pitch," similarly to the HR Snare Drum, is created by the velocity of the air being expelled.

🔊 Example #20: The Word "Kick" and the Beginning of the Word "Kick"

Now, just as you did with your HR Bass Drum and your HR Snare Drum, try experimenting with different vowels following the "k" sound, to figure out what sounds best or is the easiest to use for the time being. Try: Ki, Kuh, Koo, Ko, Kah.

🔊 Example #21: Ki, Kuh, Koo, Ko, Ah

Notice that whichever sound you settle on can be pitched to your liking by changing the speed of the air you're expelling, as well as the shape of your mouth.

Let's try a few patterns using what we've learned so far! Remember that as you move on to more difficult patterns, an inward HR Breath can often be substituted for a hi-hat if necessary. As we move on to these more challenging patterns, however, I will cease notating the HR Breath.

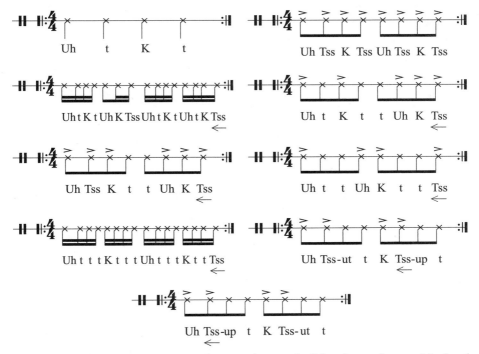

Great job! You're now ready to graduate to the wonderful and amazing world of real Vocal Percussion!

Vocal Percussion Sounds

Now that you've mastered both HR and the Gateway Sounds, you're ready to move on to the remaining Vocal Percussion sounds. The first two sounds will be the "meat" of your groove. They are the VP Bass Drum and the VP Snare Drum.

One of the most important things about using these two sounds is that they do not require any vocalization. Remember, the HR Bass Drum that you've been practicing requires a low "uh." Once you've mastered the VP Bass Drum, you will no longer be vocalizing *any* of your sounds (unless you choose to). This means you'll get less tired, you'll be able to perform longer, and you won't be trashing your vocal cords in the process, allowing you to sing later in the set while maintaining a healthier voice.

The VP Bass Drum and Snare Drum

The VP Bass Drum should be the most powerful sound you make, as it will be the driving force behind all future grooves. Typically, most Vocal Percussionists focus so much time trying to create a powerful snare drum that it often takes over their beats. A powerful snare is important; however, always do your best to keep your bass drum a little stronger and louder than your snare. This may prove difficult, as when first learning the snare drum, more air pressure and lip tension is required to get the desired snare pitch. Just be mindful and try to keep your pattern nice and balanced.

The VP Bass and Snare Drums are performed similarly. Though the VP Bass drum is a low-pitched sound and the VP Snare is a higher pitched sound, they are both made roughly the same way, by pushing air between your lips and varying their placement and tension. "The looser the lips, the sinker the ships." Just kidding. Seriously though, the looser your lips are and the further out your lower lip is, the lower the sound. Higher sounds are made oppositely, by creating more tension in the lips and keeping your lips even or allowing your upper lip to protrude a little.

These sounds will take more practice to master. But once you master them and the control of their pitches, you'll have an amazing palette of drums to choose from!

The VP Bass Drum

Bear with me for a second and try not to giggle . . . say the word "poo." I said don't giggle. Do you hear the percussive nature of the word? Say it again and listen carefully. This will actually be the basis for both your VP Bass Drum and VP Snare Drum. Now, slightly put out your lower lip, as though you were pouting. Keeping your lower lip slightly over your top lip, say the word "poo" again. Notice that it now sounds more like "boo," though still retaining the percussive nature of "poo." Additionally, pay attention to the pitch of your Bass Drum. If you want to hear the actual pitch you're producing, simply put your finger in your ear and plug it. This makes it easier to hear the resonance of your drum within your head.

Practice this sound over and over, experimenting with slight pitch variations, air velocity, and "openness" in the mouth and throat (lowering and raising the larynx to create more or less space inside your mouth). This experimentation is what will help you truly find the right and best sounds for you.

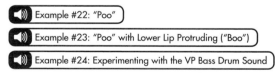

Now, for notational purposes, it is easiest to simply use the letter "B" to represent your VP Bass Drum. Let's try a few simple patterns and work our way up to adding what we've learned thus far. Remember to start slow!

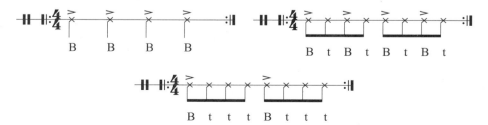

Now try adding your HR Snare.

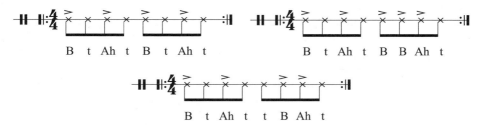

If you replace that HR Snare with the VP Rim Shot, you'll have your very first strictly VP pattern. Give it a try!

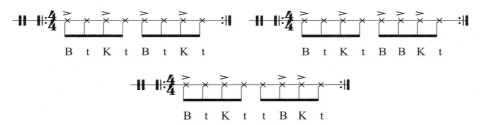

Shall we try sixteenth notes?

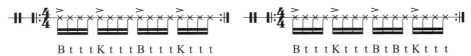

Now let's get really crazy! Try adding your VP Open Hi-Hat, the Inward VP Open Hi-Hat, and a few Sound Extensions.

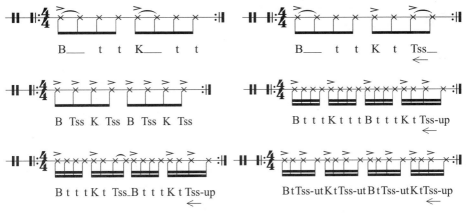

I think you're getting the hang of it! Let's move on to the VP Snare Drum.

The VP Snare Drum

As I mentioned before, the word "poo" is the basis for the VP Snare Drum as well as the VP Bass Drum. Although this sound can be a little more challenging to master, it's pretty straight forward. Say the word "poo" again. Now, keeping your lips together fairly tightly, let the pressure build behind your lips and explode in a loud and short "poo." The VP Snare is all about the pressure and tension of your lips. More than likely, your lips will need to be about even to get the desired snare drum pitch. But as always, please take the time to experiment with different tensions and mouth shapes in order to find your favorite sound.

I chose this word to teach you the snare for a good reason—it will allow for a better and faster mastering of pitch control of your snare than other options. For example, a lot of people describe the VP Snare Drum as a "pf" sound. I believe this removes the focus from the pitch of the snare and puts the emphasis on the rattle of the snares (or little metal chains) underneath the drum. Besides, when you use the word "poo," the snare rattle automatically happens when you extend the length of the word. Give it a shot, just to help drive this point home. Truthfully, whatever helps you master the VP Snare is what you should do. Just remember that learning to control the pitch will give you that extra something that most Vocal Percussionist don't have—a variety of sounds. Also, please keep in mind that this sound is probably the most difficult to master. Be patient and don't overdo it!

Side note: Your cheeks will get very sore from practicing your VP Snare Drum. Nothing is wrong with you! It's just like smiling too much.

🔊 Example #25: "Poo"

🔊 Example #26: Pressure "Poo"

🔊 Example #27: Experimenting with Pitch

🔊 Example #28: "Pf"

🔊 Example #29: Comparing "Pf" and "Poo" Snares

Alright, let's try adding the VP Snare to our practice patterns! I notate it just as I've taught it to you. Notating it as "poo" will remind you of how to produce the sound, and keeps your mouth in a good position to quickly move on to your next sound.

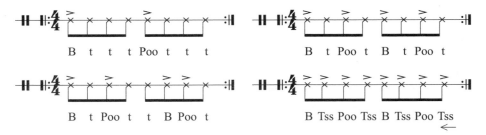

B   t   t   t Poo t   t   t   B   t Poo t   B   t Poo t

B   t Poo t   t   B Poo t   B Tss Poo Tss B Tss Poo Tss

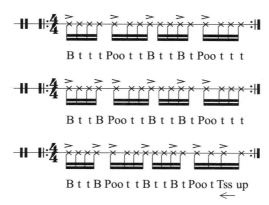

Too easy? Let's make it harder!

B t t t Poo t t B t t B t Poo t t t

B t t B Poo t t B t t B t Poo t t t

B t t B Poo t t B t t B t Poo t Tss up

Congratulations, the hard work is done! That is, until you get to the advanced patterns on www.jakemoulton.com. But for now, you have everything you need to add a solid beat to your ensemble. If you stopped here, you'd still be in great shape! But there are a few more sounds I'd like to discuss before moving on to other chapters.

Cymbals

Most people know what cymbals are—flat metal discs that you can either hit together or individually with a drumstick or mallet. Typically, they make a loud, bright crashing sound. Drummers often use them to emphasize moments in a song. They will play the same role for you. For big moments in a particular pattern or song, the VP Crash Cymbal will add another level of depth and musicality to your beat.

The VP Crash Cymbal

The VP Crash Cymbal is quite easy to make by itself. Try saying the word "cushy." Now, let's spell it with a "k" and remove the "u" and the "y." You're left with "ksh." Try saying that. Once again, try experimenting with different mouth shapes and velocity of air. Also, keep in mind that as you want the "pitch" of your cymbal to go higher, you must create less space in your mouth and change the sound slightly from "ksh" to "keesh" to "kiss" and then finally to "kss." Listen to the audio samples and then try it for yourself.

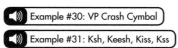

🔊 Example #30: VP Crash Cymbal

🔊 Example #31: Ksh, Keesh, Kiss, Kss

Now that you've learned the VP Crash Cymbal, I'm going to ask you to forget it. You see, you won't have much use for a crash cymbal by itself. Adding this style of crash into your groove will make it sound awkward and a little empty. Furthermore, many Vocal Percussionists like to use a "psh" sound instead.

🔊 Example #32: "Psh" Crash Cymbal

This adds a little more depth to the sound, but still lacks the emphasis that your cymbal requires. Real drummers often accentuate a crash cymbal with a bass drum. In my opinion, you should almost *always* do this. It will add more realism and musicality to your pattern and sound far more impressive. Lucky for you, it's a simple sound to make. All you need to do is add an "sh" to your VP Bass Drum. Easy! Try saying it: "bsh." Your lower lip should be protruding as you make your VP Bass Drum sound; however, at the end of the sound, you must open your mouth into a smile. Clench your teeth together and part your lips. Now say the "sh" part of the sound. Perfect. When you combine the two sounds together, you get a low bass drum coupled with a bright, high-pitched crash cymbal.

🔊 Example #33: VP Bass Drum/VP Crash Cymbal Combination

Let's try this in a simple pattern. To fully grasp the placement of the "bsh" crash, I'll write out the repeat of the pattern as well. Notice that the crash is on the downbeat of the second bar.

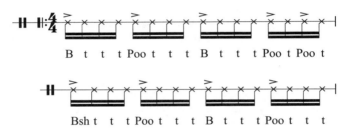

B t t t Poo t t t B t t t Poo t Poo t

Bsh t t t Poo t t t B t t t Poo t t t

Can you hear how it's supposed to be used? It's all about the accent, so it works most anywhere you need emphasis. Let's try one more for good measure.

B t t t Poo t t Bsh t t Bsh t Poo t t t

Tom-Toms and Fills

I suppose it's possible to teach style. However, I *don't* believe it's possible to teach style and stylistic fills verbally and in just a few short sentences. Tom-tom fills can be both simple and tricky. Not only must you work on mastering the appropriate tom-tom sounds for your mouth, you must also use them musically and tastefully, so as not to confuse, distract from your beat, or more importantly, distract from your group. For this reason, I will touch on the making of the sounds and provide a few simple fill patterns, but will leave the remaining lessons to the advanced techniques section of my website.

There are a few schools of thought on tom-toms. A lot of Vocal Percussionists use the words "toom" or "doom" to create their tom-tom sounds. Some of them sound great. And, honestly, my tom-toms vary only slightly. I prefer to use tom-toms sparingly in my work. I also believe in making them as realistic as possible, while also making my mouth work as efficiently as possible. (Once again, understand that if you find something that works better for you, you should use it. It's all about the individual!)

Listen to the samples of the words "toom" and "doom." In these examples, also listen to the pitches of the sounds. Tom-toms are typically tuned in fourths. But please do not obsess about this. They don't have to be in the same key as the song you're performing and they don't have to be in perfect fourths. Relax and have fun!

🔊 Example #34: Tom-Toms: "Toom"

🔊 Example #35: Tom-Toms: "Doom" Inward and Outward

Now for my technique. Keeping your mouth closed, try to recreate the feeling of holding back a smile. The corners of your mouth will tighten as your face muscles fight between smile and frown. Now, with the tip of your tongue gently resting on the back of your upper teeth, say the word "doo" or "too." The tongue will pull away from your teeth on the "oo" and you'll have to slightly open your jaw to allow the pulse of air to pop out. Try this and repeat until it really makes sense to you. You can hear the desired un-pitched sound in the following audio sample:

🔊 Example #36: VP Tom-Toms (Un-Pitched)

Repeat this sound over and over, experimenting with the addition of pitch and practicing your intervals of perfect fourths. Try not to close the sound off into an "m." Keep the air flowing, but let the pitch quickly trail off.

🔊 Example #37: VP Tom-Toms

Now let's try a few simple practice fill patterns with what we know so far! We'll be notating the tom-toms using the word "doo," so as not to confuse them with your VP Hi-Hat. Also, remember to experiment with the pitches of your tom-toms. As notating their actual pitches would be a little difficult and remove any spontaneity from your fills, I'm going to leave that completely up to you! Also, if there is a (sh) following the downbeat, use it on all the repeats, but not the original downbeat.

🔊 Example #38: Simple Tom-Tom Fills

B(sh)t t tPoo t t B t t tPoo t doo doo

B(sh)t t t Poo t t dooB t t t Poo t doo doo

B(sh)t t t Poo t t t B t doo t t doo t doo

B(sh)t t t Poo t doo doo B(sh)t t doo Poo doo B doo

I'm sure you see how notating tom-toms and drums can get REALLY confusing! Practice these patterns and then try creating some on your own!

VP Brushes

Ah, brushes, sweet brushes. I can't begin to tell you how brushes have saved me from musical death. Having studied jazz and been a big fan for a very long time, few things are more frustrating that hearing a swing VP Hi-Hat pattern accompanying a vocal jazz arrangement. In my experience, not only are the jazz hi-hat patterns distracting, they also lack "movement" and musicality. When I first taught myself the VP Brushes, it opened up a whole to world to me, and I'd like to share that with you. Now there's a trick to this . . . you don't ever really get to breathe in, like you do with the VP Inward Open Hi-Hat. Often times, you'll have to sneak a breath in a break or use a simple HR Breath so as to keep this pattern going. And it's an exhausting one. The reason is that in order to keep the realism, you must continuously breath out on an "ff." Try it: make a light "ff" sound and hold it for as long as you can. This is your continuous brush.

🔊 Example #39: Continuous Brush: "Ff"

In a slow 4/4 tempo, try holding your Continuous Brush and pulsing on beats 1 and 3.

🔊 Example #40: Continuous Brush: Pulsing on Beats 1 and 3

Great, you're halfway there! If you simply accent beats 2 and 4 lightly with your tongue with a "tf" sound, you will have your very first slow brush groove! Remember to keep your continuous brush going! That means you have to push a little extra air through when using your accent brush. Listen to the following example and practice until you've got it.

🔊 Example #41: Simple Brush Pattern/Adding Accent Brush

The pattern will look like this:

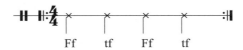

Ff   tf   Ff   tf

Now, remember what I said earlier about capitalizing to show accents? This will *really* come in handy when notating the VP Brushes. Keeping in mind that your continuous brush almost never breaks, try the following pattern and see what you come up with:

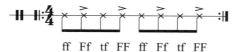

ff Ff tf FF ff Ff tf FF

How does it sound? Like this?

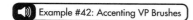

Example #42: Accenting VP Brushes

Do you remember how to notate the extension of a sound? Using an underscore. This is actually most useful when using your VP Brushes. Try this:

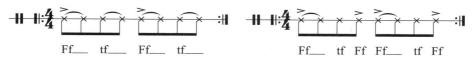

Ff__ tf__ Ff__ tf__   Ff__ tf Ff Ff__ tf Ff

How about this one?

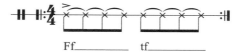

Ff_____ tf_____

Strangely enough, the previous pattern *could* sound exactly like the following, if you perform it at a slow tempo:

Ff   tf   Ff   tf

What's the difference? Subdivision.

Adding HR and VP to Brush Pattern

You're almost there! All you have to do now is add your HR and VP sounds to your brush grooves!

As the HR sounds are a bit simpler, they can actually be added and notated without much thought. Simply notate the pattern by placing your desired HR Bass Drum and HR Snare Drum in the pattern as you'd normally do.

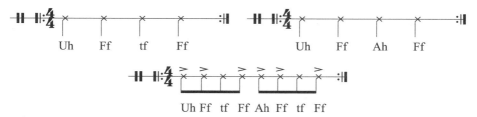

Uh   Ff   tf   Ff   Uh   Ff   Ah   Ff

Uh Ff tf Ff Ah Ff tf Ff

However, when adding your VP Bass and Snare Drums, as well as your VP Rim Shot, a few slight adjustments are necessary, and I do mean slight. All you really have to do is add a "ff" to the end of your bass drum and rim shot and choose to use your "Pf" Snare.

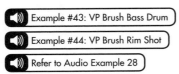

Just as you added the "ff" to the production of your sounds, you'll also add it to the notation. Your bass drum will become a "Bf", your rim shot will become a "Kf" and, obviously, your snare will be a "Pf."

Let's try a few last practice patterns before moving on!

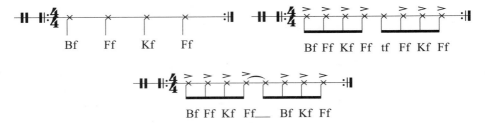

You're getting it!!

Now What?

Wow. So much information in such a tiny place. You've learned how to start from nothing and create and teach others to make some pretty cool grooves that can stretch across many styles of music. With a little practice your sense of time will become better, your vocal percussion sounds will become more realistic, and you'll start to get comfortable enough to start creating your very own patterns.

So where do you go from here? It really depends on you. If your interest in vocal percussion stops at being able to accompany your group or choir or teach someone to do just that, you may have all the tools you need. If you're like me and are completely fascinated by the art form and by the human body's ability to produce and reproduce amazing sounds, then you're just beginning your journey.

What you've learned in this chapter offers a very strong base for any vocal percussionist. The rest is almost entirely up to you. Every concert you go to, every song you listen to, and every other vocal percussionist you come across has something to offer. There is *always* something to learn and something to practice. I don't care who you are . . . there is always more to learn.

SUMMARY

» Start slowly and take your time.

» Have fun and don't take yourself too seriously.

» Work on the sounds as presented and then find a way to make them your own.

» Whenever you have the opportunity, integrate your own sounds into some of these patterns.

» Experiment.

» Don't compare yourself to others, but always be open to learning from them.

» Always be willing to share your knowledge with others.

CHAPTER 13

WHAT ABOUT THE BASS?

with Trist Curless

In this chapter, we'll spend a little time discussing what could be the most important part of your a cappella group—the bass section. As we move forward, I'll simply say "the bass" because whether you have one singer on a microphone or a group of four basses together, they are filling the role of the bass guitar in your vocal band. Remember, even ladies' groups have the lowest voice part filling this bass role.

What Is the Role of the Bass?

The bass is incredibly important because it serves two functions. The bass is the primary timekeeper for your group. I know that's a shock to most people. Many mistakenly assume that the vocal percussionist (drummer) is the timekeeper. That's simply not true. Because the bass is also your tonal anchorman, your entire group will need to tune to the bass. The bass lays down the *harmonic rhythm* of the song, meaning it generally outlines the movement of the chords.

So . . . How Many Basses Should You Have?

It depends. My answer is one, three, or four. It comes down to whether your group will have a microphone for each singer or not. In a smaller group where everyone has their own microphone, you should only have one bass. You can turn them up in the mix to balance the group, and then they can really "play the bass line" without any worries about matching another singer. Imagine a big band jazz orchestra. No matter how many horns you count, have you ever seen more than one bass? In a rock band, there might be a lead guitar and several rhythm guitars, but only one bass.

However, if you have a larger group that is using zone microphones, you should have several basses. Bass frequencies don't carry as far as treble frequencies, so all things being equal and without amplification, the treble clef is going to outbalance the bass clef unless you are careful. Having three or even four basses is a good idea. I once had a group with two basses—never again. It was a nightmare getting them to match. Even though matching four basses is difficult, the fact that there's more of them leads any non-matching to balance out, if you get my drift. It's much like developing blend in a choir. I've always found it easiest to get a nice blend with three singers or more.

To Mic or Not to Mic?

If you have one bass on a microphone . . .

. . . use the proximity effect of your hand-held mic to boost bass frequencies. With most hand-helds, the closer the voice to the microphone, the richer and more bass-y the sound becomes. With this in mind, many basses will "eat the mic," or keep the microphone head very close to their lips. Some will even place the microphone between the top of their mouth and their nose in order to use "nose air" to create a sound. That's really a personal preference, and simply requires some play time to figure out what works for your bass.

. . . let the microphone do the work for you. Many basses will try to fully resonate each tone as if they are singing solo. This can cause some unnatural sounds, especially in the low end. There's no need to force out sound—you're on a mic! Simply sing each pitch comfortably and articulate well. Let the mic do the work for you.

. . . adjust your syllable approach. After all, a single bass on a mic is trying to replicate a bass guitar. Last time I checked, bass guitars do not ever sound like "doom-bop-pa mow mow." Almost all bass syllables in this style will be a neutral "thm," with the "th" added to give some definition to the rhythm. Occasionally, use a "b" or "d" sound to create accents in the bass line. On rare occasions, add an open vowel for a large accent. Of course, when the bass sings lyrics in a homophonic choral section or as a solo line, they'll need to switch gears drastically. They'll need to pull the microphone out a bit when opening up to words, or else the sound will likely be over-driven.

If you have a section of basses . . .

. . . make sure they match. Most sections of your a cappella group will bounce back and forth between instrument sounds, syllables, pure vowels on long tones, and lyrics (for harmonies and echoes). The bass section will almost always work with instrument replacement sounds. You might need to alter syllables that are closed (thm-dm) in order to create more sound. Think back to Chapter 6 **Turkey Bacon**, where we went from open syllables to a "sound." Can you reverse this process if needed to open up your bass section?

| DM | DUHM | DOME | DOH |
| THM | THUM | THAWM | THAW |

Remember, a bass line can sound hokey in a heartbeat if not handled well, so only open the line in order to balance the group sonically.

. . . balance the volume of the ensemble around them, not the other way around. Your basses can only sing so loud. That's a fact. You are certainly more likely to achieve success if you balance the sound of your group to your basses than if you continually ask the basses to give more and more.

. . . try using a baritone line to help the cause. The natural reinforcement of overtones begins with an octave, then with the interval of a perfect fifth. If you need more bass than you have (as high schools often do), try using baritones or second tenors in your arrangements to sing parallel fifths with the bass for strength. Granted, you shouldn't do this throughout an entire song, but if you need a section with more punch, this can help a lot.

An Interview with Trist Curless (Bass of m-pact)

Because the bass is such a unique creature, I wanted to get an expert's advice on how to best handle playing the role of bass in an a cappella setting. Trist was nice enough to talk with me about the subject, and the transcript of that discussion follows for us to enjoy. **My questions are in bold** and *Trist's answers are in italics.* Thanks so much, Trist!

There is often a shortage of true basses in the high school setting. How low do you need to be able to sing to be a bass in pop a cappella?

That depends on your arrangements. Are you going to depend on stock arrangements you get from someone else? If so, it can be more work. You're almost better off arranging for the people you have. That isn't always feasible based on your timeline, budget and skill-set. The first preference would be to arrange all the stuff yourself. Then if you don't have sopranos who are too high or basses who are too low, you're okay. The second choice would be to alter existing arrangements to accommodate your ranges. Choice 2a would be to use some technology. A bass octave pedal can help a baritone achieve low bass notes if used well, but it does take some practice to make it sound natural. Look at your own situation and know that there is no rule book. Start by thinking, "Here's what we have and here's where we want to go . . . So how do we get there?"

Find out what your bass' lowest note is and don't write below it.

For an individual bass, let the mic do all the work. Get your system set properly and then you only have to get the sound into the mic. Don't sing so hard; turn the mic up. Singing bass with a mic should be all air. Air, air, air, air, air!

What is the difference between singing individual bass and singing in a bass section?

It's rare that I hear a section of basses that really pulls it off. It's just a lot more work. It depends on the song. In ballads, the bass singer is usually the "singer" of the lowest part rather than a performer with the mindset of a bass player, therefore singing with more than one person is no different from any other part, so that kinda works. In a swing tune, it would be really hard to match. You don't ever see two string bass players together, do you? At least not very often in jazz, pop, or funk tunes.

What are some things that bass singers should know about interpreting syllables so they sound authentic rather than square?

To me, it's totally in the same conversation as jazz improvisation with syllables. To me, with scat singing, you know you're kinda there when you stop thinking about what the syllables are. The syllables are completely unimportant to you. You're thinking about what the music is, and you're actually thinking of melodic things to do. When that is your focus, there's no way for you to think about "what the words are." When you're thinking about what the music is, the way to get it out will do it itself.

If you're not so worried about tone, if you're really relaxed and thinking about what the bass line is, you won't make square sounds. If you're thinking about what the music does, you just can't. That's a little bit out there, but if you break it down, it's mostly tone-driven.

As a bass player, I usually use a "thm" without much "th" on it . . . Just enough to give it something more than a hum. Your accents might have an extra "b" or "d." What better way to accent than to add a more open syllable?

If you have more than one bass, you would literally have to write out where everyone changes. It doesn't really matter which way it goes if everybody does it. When there are syllables in an arrangement, the first thing you have to decide is, "Will MY guys sound good singing that?" You need to adapt the music for your situation.

Should you consider a bass octave pedal?

If the music has that feel, then sure. It should be driven from a desire to deliver the music better, not a desire to play with toys.

What are some tips on microphone technique?

You are using the bass proximity of the microphone to your advantage. Just turn one on and talk into it, then move it closer and closer to your mouth. You'll quickly find out how the bass response works in the mic. Most of the time the microphone basically rests on my lips.

Summary

» The bass section is your timekeeper.

» Use one bass or three or more in a section.

» Individual basses should neutralize their syllables and use the microphone's proximity effect to bring out low frequencies.

» Multiple basses should open their syllables and match them across the section.

» Balance the volume of the group to the bass section, not the other way around.

» Use baritone parts on parallel fifths to add extra punch if needed.

CHAPTER 14

The Solo Vocalist:
Techniques, Tips, and Tricks
To Tell the Tale
with Nate Altimari

In this chapter I will highlight some of the attributes that every good soloist utilizes. Some of these may be simple, common sense notions and some may be things that you never thought of. In my years as a vocalist I have found that few, if any, of the following should be treated as optional. Every vocalist can learn to be better, and my hope is to help guide you towards that goal.

Breathing: *Not Just for Living Anymore*

Perhaps the simplest (and yet largely underestimated) concept is the role of breath control. Is it truly as simple as it seems? Proper breathing is what allows us to sing in tune (pitch), in time (rhythm), in multiple octaves (range), multiple volumes (dynamics), and most importantly, in ways that are pleasing to be heard (style). The true proper breath should never move your shoulders or expand your chest-cavity. It should never be drawn in through your nose or clenched-teeth, and most of all; it should never be completely exhausted before it is replenished. Try the following exercise:

1. Lie on your back, as if you were standing to sing, with feet shoulder-width apart, arms loosely placed at your sides, and head looking straight ahead (or in this case, up).

2. Place a textbook-sized book on your stomach, below your ribcage. On that book place a rounded object, like a tennis ball or an apple.

3. Slowly purge your lungs, and then take a full breath, slowly, through an open mouth.

What happened? If you're like most of us, the tennis ball or apple rolled toward your pant-line because your lungs expanded outward, causing your chest to rise, tipping the book. Now, try the same exercise again, but this time, imagine your stomach expanding like a balloon—evenly, in all directions. This is easier said than done, so don't get frustrated and think, "I don't know how to breathe well." It will come. The goal is for the book to rise evenly (to be level) without disturbing the tennis ball or apple. If you can do this, you are on your way to proper breath control. Singers and instrumentalists must always "breathe from the diaphragm," which is what you just did. Your diaphragm is one of the strongest muscles in your body. Why not use it to draw breath in and push breath out?

Another way to strengthen your breathing technique requires a partner. Have another person hold their arms out (elbows locked) with their body braced to support your weight. Lean forward until your abdominal muscles are against the closed fists, your body approaching a 45-degree angle. While you are in this position, sing an exercise or a difficult phrase from your solo. In order to keep a consistent sound, you will have to keep consistent tension in your core, both while breathing in and breathing out.

While this method is extreme, it will very quickly help you identify the source of your breath control. From that point forward, you can place your hands on your abs while you are singing, feel that tension, and keep it there. As you learn to control your breath, you will find that you can sing louder (and quieter), longer (and shorter), brighter (and darker), higher (and lower), more in tune, and more in time. Every aspect of your singing will improve.

Projection

One of the biggest challenges we face in a cappella groups, especially in standard high school and collegiate style a cappella groups, is being heard over our ensemble. Of course, this isn't entirely our responsibility as a soloist (the background singers have to be sensitive), but we are certainly required to do our part. By projecting our voice, we *can* be heard over the group. Projection is one of many functions of breathing. Proper use of breath will allow the singer to focus their airflow to achieve many different levels of volume. (Note: singing quietly requires significantly more air than singing loudly.)

Often times, students struggle with finding their "belting" voice—that loud, crisp, bright (yet still pretty) sound that Broadway singers utilize frequently. The truth is, we use that part of our voice often, and we just don't know it. An example might be

trying to get someone's attention from across a football field or shouting at your annoying brother for going through your stuff, or catching the dog on the sofa. This full-breathed, loud, clear yell (while not an angry yell) is that same part of your voice. No, of course you are not aiming to yell your solo, but harnessing that part of your voice and using that resonance is the key to great projection—and full breathing is the first step.

Sustain, Sustain (I Know Your Name)

Sometimes we are required to sing long notes—it's just the truth. Whether it's in a background part, the sweeping climactic bridge of a rock anthem, or the chorus of a beautiful passionate ballad, long notes happen. Pacing your breathing will help you achieve maximum sustain without losing pitch or volume. There are two steps to this. One is using proper inhalation technique, while the other is creating a focused stream of air as you sing.

> *Efficient Inhalation*: Imagine you are holding an empty paper towel tube in front of your mouth (or hold your hand in the shape of an "O" approximately as wide). Now, open your mouth to match the size of that opening and slowly breathe in. Notice how your lungs fill up and your stomach expands (see above) much more efficiently. Now, try the same technique, but this time, after purging your breath, take one strong, short breath through the same wide opening. What did you notice? If you did it right, you'll note that your stomach expanded again, but that even in a short amount of time, you managed to draw in an incredible amount of air. This is the same technique that tuba players use. Tuba players are lucky if they get eight beats worth of music out of one lung full of air, but often times are required to sound for much longer. They utilize this breathing technique to get maximum air in minimum time, avoiding gaping holes in the music.

> *Controlled Exhalation*: Imagine that your air stream is the diameter of a pencil. Close your lips to the width of a pencil and slowly but forcefully expel all of the air in your lungs. You should be able to exhale in this fashion for quite a while. This is the type of airstream you should use as you sing, whether loud or soft, short or long. A focused stream of air (created by tensing your abdominal muscles) will result in consistent tone, consistent pitch, and consistent volume (projection).

If you can master these few ideas, you will be well on your way to a more consistent solo voice. You will find that your voice will strengthen and in time your range could expand (which seems to be the one thing almost ALL singers want). Keep at it and challenge yourself—you'll get there.

Healthy Singing in the "Pop Style"
(Or *How Not to Mess Things Up in There*)

As most vocalists will tell you, singing in the pop or rock style is very different from singing traditional classical or choral music. The most noticeable difference is the tension that is often present in the pop/rock voice. Many rock stars sing with horrible technique. While it is important to sound "authentic" when singing pop music, it is important not to short-cut technique and claim a right to unhealthy singing under the excuse of "style." There may be pop singers who are making millions singing poorly, risking their vocal health for a place in the spotlight. But unlike these rare creatures, you won't have all those millions of dollars to ease the pain of a damaged voice if you aren't careful with your performances.

So how should choral singers approach the world of pop to sound good and stay healthy? Knowing your own abilities is a good start. You must exhibit self-control, keeping yourself in check. Being aware of any discomfort you may feel is important. If anyone ever tells you that a sore throat is part of your voice getting stronger, or that you are building calluses, they are wrong. Calluses by definition are rough, hardened spots that are less flexible than normal tissue, and your vocal chords are very tender, soft pieces of tissue. You want to imagine *massaging* those muscles. Tenderize them; make them more pliable. The best exercise for this is properly warming up. There's no two ways about it. You may know singers who don't warm up, or perhaps just give their throats a good gruff clearing and say, "There, I'm warm." The truth is, unless you talk really high, low, and in between all day (please, tell me you don't do this), you are only using a fraction of your vocal chords and definitely need to warm up. If you are a teacher reading this book, you fully understand the need (and exercises) for warming up. If you are a student, use the warm-ups given you by your private teacher or choir director.

Once you are warmed up, you're ready to work on your solo. What is most important is to stay resonant and keep your voice freely produced. When rock singers abuse their voices, they are trying to create tension and excitement in the sound. They want their voices to sound full of passion and effort. Trained singers use resonance to create a similar excitement without over-taxing the vocal mechanism.

If your voice is resonant, it will be exciting. You can then incorporate pop stylings that do not undermine your technique. Pop singers often bend pitch or slide across intervals. They will sing with impure vowels. They add "runs" to longer notes to add soul to their solos. You can do all these things, too. And remember, what is a "run" anyway? It's really an ornamentation. Pop runs are just slightly sloppy melismas. We will elaborate on these stylings towards the end of this chapter when we discuss *embellishment*.

Range: Know It. Expand It.

Knowing your range is an important part of singing safely. It may be the first step to singing healthily, so as not to damage those soft little vocal chords you have. In time you *can* expand your range, but for now, let's work on strengthening what you've got.

Settling into your range, your *full*-voice range, is fundamentally easy. It's the voice you use most, the voice with which you're most comfortable. Still, soloists often sing outside their range because they fall in love with a song and they just want to sing it. Maybe the song has just a few notes that are dicey, so they think, "I can do that *sometimes*. I'll grow into it." If you're *really close,* maybe you will grow into it. If not, maybe pick another song. After all, there are a lot of songs out there, right?

It is important to remember when picking a solo that your range isn't always the same. Our bodies are in constant fluctuation due to health, amount of sleep, hydration, and the like. On top of that, if your group sings sharp or flat a half step because they're having a rough night, you might end up with notes you didn't think you'd have to sing. Remember these tips for solo range consideration:

» Don't sing a solo unless you know you can sing it well *all* the time, even if your voice isn't quite 100%. If you can't sing all the notes healthfully all the time, pick another song (or transpose it depending on the arrangement and how that fits your group).

» Don't just check the top and bottom notes. Check the tessitura. Some songs just hang high for a long time. You have to have enough stamina to sing the whole song without becoming fatigued. Time and time again, student soloists have chosen songs that work well until the last third of the song, then their quality begins to buckle under the strain of repetition.

» If the solo has a repeated chorus that has many strenuous notes, it would be fair to improvise over some of the repeats to avoid the fatigue (and monotony) factor.

» Check out "gender bender" songs. Some songs originally sung by a high tenor can be sung by a low alto. Songs that were sung by higher female voices could be done in the baritone octave.

Presenting Your Solo:
Does It Make Sense Emotionally AND Visually?

I can't tell you how many times I've heard a soloist and thought, "What is your song about?" It happens all the time. I hear a soloist and find myself distracted by the lack of connection between the soloist and the song they are singing. Classical singers translate the texts of their foreign language songs in order to become aware of the song's story. Why wouldn't you pay attention to such things while singing in English? It seems like common sense, doesn't it? Yet many soloists never bother. I'll break down the following into a few sections.

Emotionally Conveying Your Story

How may times have we seen groups performing gorgeous songs, for instance, "I Can't Make You Love Me" by Bonnie Raitt, with a dippy grin, smiling eyes, and too much body movement? Is there anything more distracting or stomach turning? When you are on stage, in front of your group, and singing for an audience of *any* size, your job is that of an actor (to some extent). We all know that "I Can't Make You Love Me" is a sad song. But is it *just* a sad song? It's a song about a woman (or man) fighting to set aside their understanding that this relationship is over in order to survive one more passionate night with their lover. Could it be that the content could be construed as hopeful, even if just momentarily?

If you've ever felt love and lost, then you can't help but be destroyed by this. So, how do you convey this to your listener? In a live setting, think about what the words mean to *you*. Does this song remind you of some emotional moment in your life? Is there a moment you can drum up in your mind that helps you feel something akin to the subject? Find that, focus on it, and let it control how you perform this song. Nothing impacts your audience more than connecting with them by breaking down emotional walls, showing yourself, and making it seem real . . . for you.

Visually Conveying the Right Message

How are you holding yourself? Are you swaying your hips, tapping your feet, snapping your fingers, popping your head, subdividing the beat in your head (AND body)? This is a common error for soloists. As the lead, you are *not* responsible for showing or driving the beat, and in terms of a ballad, you should move as little as possible. Nothing is more poignant than a singer standing stark still, stone-faced, stoically delivering a heart-wrenching ballad. So in short, your voice, your face, and your stance all are part of performing a solo. I'm not saying you shouldn't show that you are with the music—James Brown never stops moving, but he's not just standing there tapping his foot, keeping rhythm. You have the luxury of being the front man (or woman) for your song, so make good use of it.

The key is making sure there is a connection between your song and it's emotional content, and the way you are holding yourself. In terms of up-tempo, happy tunes, the same can be said—you wouldn't stand still with your hands in your pockets while you are singing "Get Ready" by the Temptations, would you? If you did, the audience would chuck tomatoes at you. I know I would. Your job as an actor in this case is to engage the audience in a different way—to show them how happy you are, what this song means to you, and infect them with that happiness.

Lastly, the same emotive notion can be implemented with your full group as well. If your group is performing the previously-mentioned Bonnie Raitt tune, and you are doing everything right (somber, hopeful, and anguished face, emotional almost sobbing-voice, and stoic stance), but your ensemble is bopping back and forth, smiling and laughing with each other, conveying a party, then the effect is completely gone. At that point, it doesn't matter what *you* do, your group has ruined the effect for you. The same can be said for up-tempo songs. The group is as responsible for conveying the tone of the songs as the lead. For "Get Ready," the ensemble *should* be having fun, engaging each other and the audience, and making the audience wish they were on stage with them.

This type of emotional/visual unity is called the *capsule concept*. For a full description of the capsule concept, see Chapter 10 **Your Visual Plan**. That chapter discusses the nature of the capsule concept and how to create it with your group. But as the soloist, it is important to understand that you are (a) the number one projector of the capsule concept and (b) the most important vote in what the capsule concept is. You are the one who has to sell this song. You have to be in an honest, emotional state of mind. You have to set the capsule concept, communicate it to your group, and allow them to support your vision of the song.

The Value of Emulation

Soloist Emulation

A cappella music (at least on the scholastic level) is largely comprised of "cover tunes," meaning performances of existing songs. Some a cappella groups write their own music, but most tend to cover other artists' material. It makes sense—audiences like the familiar. When we are singing other people's songs, however, it is easy to fall into the trap of emulating the original artist. This can range from simply singing the notes and phrasing exactly like the recording to actually manipulating your voice to sound like the original artist.

Unfortunately, more often than not the singer who attempts to sound like the original artist misses the mark. Not many of us can sound like David Lee Roth from Van Halen or Steven Tyler from Aerosmith, but that doesn't stop us from trying. Why? Shouldn't we want to sing with our own voice? After all, voices are like snowflakes: *no two are alike.* You'll never (and I mean never) be a better Whitney Houston than Whitney Houston. Have you also considered that Whitney Houston couldn't have been a better you than you? This glorious truth is one of the best parts about being a singer. *No one sings like you.*

How/When to Improvise the Melody Line
(Or *Sing It The Same? Sing It Different!*)

This is another favorite topic: expanding on the idea of the original melody line by improvisation. As "cover artists" it is common to stick to the original melody of the song, because we know it works. We sing these songs because we like them, just the way they are. In order to make a cover song your own, try these tips:

1. Learn the song note-for-note from the original and capture the feeling, the original intent.

2. Allow yourself to explore embellishments in small increments throughout the song.

3. Be aware of the new choices you are making, remember them, and over time, create a new "map" for the song that includes some of your own twists and turns (and maybe even some new material).

Listening to live performances by your favorite artists is a great way to hear how changing things up in the melody can add to (and unfortunately, sometimes detract from) the performance. It is fair to assume that as the artist was writing the song, way back when it was just an idea, there were initial melodic ideas. It is also safe to assume that over time, as the artist practiced, performed, and eventually recorded the song, these melodic ideas changed. The artist probably started adding little riffs, some melodic expansion, maybe some chordal changes to allow for these changes. Music develops organically.

As cover artists, we are likely most familiar with an already-developed version of a song. In some cases, we know both studio and live versions and have incorporated some elements from each into our own solo performance. This is where the original artist's performance stops and our own "original" interpretation begins.

As far as a basic formula for expanding on a solo, here is what I typically recommend (and also utilize when I am performing cover material):

1. Start by being faithful to the original material, through the first verse and chorus. This will establish familiarity to the audience—that moment when the audience can say, "Oh yeah! We love this song!"

2. By the second verse, it is safe to add a bit here and there, just a sprinkling of new material. Keep the general feel and melody of the song intact. This is the moment when the audience starts thinking, "I knew I liked this song, but I really like this version. How unique!"

3. As you approach the bridge, there are two options. For some listeners, the bridge is the most memorable part of a song. Typically it is climactic, the only melodic idea that is never repeated, and often times it will resolve some of the lyrical content. For these reasons, it might prove worthwhile to stick with the original bridge material. However, you could also completely reinvent the bridge and make it your own.

4. As you return to the final choruses of the song, my personal preference is to try some new material. Add something, maybe sing a chorus up an octave (if you safely have the range) or add some runs to spice things up. That said, I think returning to the original chorus material by the end of the song is important. It reminds the listener that this is a song they know and love.

Embellishment:
Just the Right Amount of Style

Now that we've covered the theory of how to approach the embellishment of a solo, let's talk about specific techniques. These are presented in no particular order.

Runs

Runs are some of the most common solo stylings today. Runs sound like a "wiggle" of tone. They are essentially the result of moving through many notes quickly in succession on one held syllable. They are the pop music version of a melisma. In order to build good runs, you must make sure you stay within the chordal framework and sing notes within the scale. Don't expect your runs to be clean right off the bat. Start off by singing them under tempo and then work your way up to the actual speed.

Changing Range

This could be as simple as singing a phrase of the solo up or down an octave. It could be a bit more complex, such as taking a section of a melody that normally progresses up and reinventing it so that it turns down. The converse could also occur, causing a phrase to turn up at the end instead of down.

Changing Rhythm

An easy way to create some interest in a repetitive solo is to change the rhythm each time the material comes back around. This can be especially useful if the soloist sings against the background vocals (who should NOT change rhythm), creating either interlocking rhythms or rhythmic tension.

Improvisation Over a Chorus or Vamp

As cliché as it might be, let's not forget the power of simple improvisation. Something as simple as humming, nonsense words like "baby, baby," or just "yeah, yeah, yeah" can be laid over the background vocals to good effect. Also, if the song has many repeated choruses, improvisation will allow the soloist to moderate their vocal output in times of illness or vocal strain.

Summary

» Great solo singing starts and ends with the breath.

» Always warm up.

» Solid solo selection secures singing success.

» Use the *capsule concept* to steer all musical and visual plans.

» Make the solo your own.

» Embellish with a plan, allowing it to evolve through the development of the song.

Performing

CHAPTER 15

MOVING TO THE STAGE

The goal of your group is to perform. This sounds obvious, but let's just say that again. *The goal of your group is to perform.* Too often directors get hung up on perfection (trust me, I know. . .). If you wait until something is "performance ready," to perform it, then you are missing part of your improvement cycle.

Fill in the blank: Practice makes _____.

Did you write "perfect?" Sorry . . . that's not correct. Other wrong answers include "better," "great," or "good." The correct answer is "permanent." *Practice makes permanent.* Therefore, you must practice performing to make your performance abilities permanent. Performing forces the issue. We say things in rehearsal like "don't stop" or "recover quickly from your mistakes." We preach "don't let us know when you mess up" or "sell it no matter what." Without an audience, the performer always knows on some level that they have an escape hatch. Rehearsal is playing for funsies. Performance means playing for keeps.

One of the reasons groups don't perform much is simply that everyone is busy. My advice is to create performance opportunities and then trade them for rehearsal. My group rehearses Monday nights, but if we can get a Thursday gig we'll swap. The gig is just more valuable in every way. The kids get a chance to perform under pressure and practice their leadership skills as they take care of their non-musical jobs (see Chapter 21 **Creating the Culture**).

Here are some ways to create performance opportunities for your group. This list is by no means complete, since there are always new ways to find an audience. Be creative!

Hosting Your Own Show

You almost certainly have your own concerts at school, and those count for sure. In addition, have you considered creating your own show in alternate venues? Here are a few to try:

» *The Coffeehouse*: Many coffeehouses are used to having small musical acts. If you have at least twenty minutes, you can do a set at the top of each hour. The songs are the same for you, but there are different customers all night long. That gives you time in-between for self-critique and brainstorming on how to improve for the next set.

» *The Church*: Churches love to have kids perform, and it doesn't have to be sacred music. It just has to be family-friendly, which your music would be anyway as a school group. Many youth groups sponsor dinners or talent shows to raise funds for a project or mission work. Offer your singing for free and it's the start of a great relationship.

» *The Guest Artist*: A really inspiring event for your kids is to host a concert by a professional a cappella group, and then perform as the opening act at the concert. You can often get a clinic in the bargain, too! There are three good ways to handle this one:

  • *For Profit*: You'll take a risk up front, but in this scenario, you pay the guest artist and then sell your tickets (the "gate") and keep the profit.

  • *For Fun*: If you don't need the money and just want to get your kids excited, find a group who will agree to perform for the proceeds of the gate (minus expenses).

  • *Split the Gate*: This is exactly as it sounds—halfway between the previous two options.

Have Music, Will Travel

It's easier than you think to get hired to entertain local crowds. When you do "the community gig"—meaning you sing for the holiday dinner or officer installation at the local Rotary Club, Masonic Lodge, or Optimists' Club—you are not only helping your performance skills, but your community relations and your bottom line as well. Many organizations will call the high school in an attempt to be community-friendly, but you can also get some referrals by leaving business cards with the local catering halls. Announce your availability at your home concerts; many parents have community ties. My advice is to have a set fee in mind, but start by asking what their budget is. Don't get hung up on fees. You can always find a way to say no without using money as the reason. If you get to where your group is singing up a storm and you have too many offers coming in, then worry about it.

Festivals and Competitions

There are some festivals and competitions in existence right now, and more popping up each day. One of the biggest is called ICHSA—the International Competition of

High School A cappella. Groups have 12 minutes to present a show package to be scored by judges at a regional competition. Those who win their region (and those who score high enough by "wild-card" video submission) are invited to New York City for the final competition.

There are other "professional" festivals such as SingStrong, BOSS (Boston Sings), LAAF (Los Angeles A cappella Festival) and SoJam that are adding high school components.

In addition, many high schools are sponsoring their own festivals and competitions. The festival scene is evolving so fast that you'll likely need to do some internet research to stay current.

Summary

Performances are crucial to your development. Some ways to increase your performance schedule include:

» Hosting your own show (at school or in town)

» Soliciting performances from community groups

» Traveling to festivals or competitions

CHAPTER 16

Booking a Gig

One of the most important aspects of having a performing group is, well . . . performing. Whether you have an a cappella group, show choir, quartet, or chamber choir, it's important to perform often. Performances are worth ten rehearsals. They're also a lot of fun.

What Is a Gig?

A gig is a performance. More specifically, a gig is a performance for hire, even if you are hired in a no-pay capacity. Gigs are outside your school schedule of concerts. Gigs can be incredibly educational if you involve your students in the process of planning them, and if you use the opportunity to build their professionalism.

Gigs are also great to use as "real world dress rehearsals" for larger concerts or competitions. Let's say you are going to compete in the ICHSA (International Competition of High School A cappella). It would be wise to find several gigs leading up to your competition, and use them to hone your performance set. There are certain pressures inherent to performance that simply aren't present in a rehearsal:

» You are unable to stop when things begin to go wrong.

» There is an audience to engage.

» The whole set must be run fluidly, with transitions, talking, etc.

» Stamina is required to sing your whole set at once, which cannot be built by rehearsing each song on its own.

How Do You Get Gigs?

At some point, the public will search you out. Many community organizations immediately think of high school groups as entertainment for their functions. Such ensembles are affordable, and it does enhance the sense of community at their event. And if your phone isn't ringing, you can prime the pump.

Check with Churches

Many churches have youth group functions that require entertainment. It is quite possible that some of your singers are involved in these youth groups. Volunteering your services for a church fundraiser is a great way to get experience while sharing with your community.

Leave Information with Local Banquet Centers

Banquet centers play host to many community functions. Whether it is the Rotary Club luncheon or the Lion's Club holiday dinner, the first point of contact is the banquet center. Take the time to contact the manager, meet with them, and leave some business cards. Once you land a few gigs and perform successfully (and professionally), you'll find that the manager will recommend your group more and more often.

Ask Your Administration

There are many school events that are not sporting events or pep rallies. The Board of Education might enjoy some entertainment at their holiday party or even at one of their regular meetings.

Apply for Local Festivals

Many local fairs and festivals take applications for entertainment. You might have to submit an audition recording to be considered, but it's worth the effort. When you perform at such public events, you are exposing your group to many possible future clients.

Steps in the Booking Process

No matter how you get a gig offer, there are several details you must know in order to determine whether you will accept it or not. They are similar to the old journalism mantra: who, what, when, where, why (and how much).

Who

Who is asking you to perform? Make sure you not only record the name of the contact person, but the organization they represent (if any).

What

What is the nature of the performance? Are you entertainment that comes after a dinner? Are you background music for a mixer? Are you an opening act or a headliner?

Where

Where is the event to be held? It is important to know how far you must travel to determine what arrangements you must make for your students. Sometimes it is even possible to land two gigs on the same night, if the locations are convenient.

When

The date is obviously important, as is the start time of the performance. You must also remember to check the window of time in which you are to set up if you are bringing sound gear. Some gigs want you to set up the night before, or in the afternoon before people arrive. This will affect whether or not the gig is worth your time, or at least provoke some discussion with the solicitor. If you are to perform 20 minutes of music an hour away from your school, and they want you to set up four hours in advance, that might not be feasible. Don't be afraid to speak plainly and respectfully about such things. Many organizations simply don't think about your logistics. Be clear about how long it will take you to set up (you've timed it, right?) and what is a workable format, if you are travelling.

Why

This is the most important consideration when fielding a gig offer. You have to know why you are taking any given gig. In order to understand this better, you'll have to answer the question of "how much?"

How Much

How much music are they expecting? Some gigs want an hour or even two hours of music. Make sure that your repertoire matches their desires. If they want more music than you have, you'll have to decide if the gig is big enough to warrant learning extra in the time allotted, or ask them if the audience "turns over." An hour of music at an outdoor festival could turn into two sets of 30 minutes each. Advertised correctly, you could get two separate audiences.

How much money are they offering?

How much experience do you need to make a good impression?

I make gig decisions like this:

> » I ask the client what their budget is so that I have an idea before I mention a number. That way, I can explain my process without them feeling awkward about money.

> » I have a monetary value that is a "suggested donation" to the program. If the client can hit that number and my kids are free, we book the gig.

> » If the client's budget is below the target number, I find out what they would be comfortable paying and tell them that I will discuss the gig with my group internally. Many times, students want to perform regardless of the money, and if we aren't busy or are prepping for big event, we'll do the gig for the experience. If it is a busy time like Christmas, we might not need to schedule a fourth gig in a week, and we'll pass.

Above all else, remember that your performance has value. If you take gig after gig without thought of money, you could be doing your program a disservice. Your students have to give of their time and you likely have expenses (music, sound gear). It's fair to earn money that goes back into your program. When your students see that their extended efforts can lead to better circumstances for their group, they'll be more likely to gig. The more they gig, the better they'll perform, and the positive cycle continues.

Questions to Ask

Once you've accepted the gig, there are some details beyond the basics to uncover. When you call the client to accept, make sure you ask the following questions:

When will we set up?

This is critical if you have sound equipment. If you are to perform after dinner, the client might not want you to set up while dinner is served.

How much space will we have?

Make sure you have enough room for your singers. While a cappella groups generally take up less room than a show choir, 16–20 singers require a decent amount of space. If you have a smaller group, that might be less of an issue. Ask if you will be on a stage or on a flat floor. If you are on a stage, you'll need to make sure you are aware of the best way to load onto the stage.

Will you have a "green room" or "holding tank?"

There is often some dead time between your arrival and setup until you perform. Make sure they have someplace you can go in order to stay out of their way. Ask in advance if that space is far enough removed that you will be able to rehearse if you wish.

How many people will be there and of what demographic?

You should tailor your set list as much as possible to match the demographic of the crowd. If your audience is primarily senior citizens, you might cut your hip-hop number in favor of a Motown chart. If you don't have enough material to make changes in the set list, make sure you discuss your song selection with the client so they have accurate expectations of what you will be singing.

Will you have access to power?

If you have sound gear, you'll need power. Most of the time that's not a problem, but in banquet halls you need to consider where your extension cords are running. Sometimes, the client wants you to perform in an area where the power cords end up running through the servers' path. Outside gigs often require long extension cords to get to power. If there's no power available at all, you could rent a small generator.

Are you allowed to sell merchandise?

This varies by the nature of the gig. It is proper to ask in advance. Many audience members will ask if you have a CD for sale, so it's better that everyone know the protocol up front.

What happens after you perform?

Some clients have a closing speech or ceremony directly after your performance and would prefer that you wait before tearing down. Make sure you cover this so that you don't get stuck in an awkward situation.

Is the performance time flexible?

If the client tells you that you'll perform after dinner at 8:00 P.M., you should confirm that the time is set. Sometimes the start time is an estimate, and if there is a holdup with dinner service or if a speaker running long, you could be sitting on hold for an extra half-hour or more. You should allow some flexibility, but I suggest you tell the client that you will need to begin within 15 minutes of the scheduled start time.

Is this a private engagement or open to the public?

If you list your gigs on your website, you'll want to indicate whether they are public or private so that your fans know whether they can come support you. If it is a public gig, it's only right that you help promote it as you can.

What is their payment process?

Some organizations want an invoice in advance so they can pay you at the gig. Some want an invoice at the gig so they can mail you a check later. Make sure you keep track of your gigs and their payment status.

Gig Sheet

Organization: _____

Point of Contact: _____

Performance Date: _____

E-mail: _____

Phone: _____ Cell Phone: _____

Details

Location: _____

Address: _____

Meeting time for group: _____

Departure time for group: _____

Setup deadline: _____

Performance time: _____ Length of set: _____

Notes

Fee: _____

☐ Invoice required

☐ Payment at gig

☐ Payment mailed

Merchandise allowed?

☐ Yes

☐ No

Gear Needed:

☐ Mains

☐ Monitors

☐ Mics

☐ Snake

☐ Mixer

☐ Effects

Guidelines for Your Singers

Make sure your singers know that every gig is a chance to practice professionalism.

Dress is important

Plan what you will wear in advance. Will you change at the gig, or wear your outfits there? Make sure the singers have their outfits laundered in advance and look sharp.

Watch your language

When you are at a gig, you must remember you are under constant scrutiny. Of course, "watch your language" means no cursing, but it also means being aware that people are always around—servers bustle here and there; clients go in and out of the restroom. Consider that you are never really alone when on a gig. Speak respectfully at all times, using your "sir, ma'am, please, and thank you" manners. Also watch your volume, as you are likely in a place of business or near other engagements.

No horseplay—you're on the clock

High school students can get goofy if they have down time. Make sure they don't get carried away in public. Also set up a cell-phone policy. It doesn't look professional to have your singers pull out their phones every other minute to text.

Thank everyone

Gratitude is the attitude. Make sure you thank everyone, all the time. Thank the servers who help you find everything and thank the client for having you. Thank them both privately and at least once during your performance.

Always act excited and happy

As cliché as it sounds, you must be happy while on the gig. Repeatedly use phrases such as "we're so glad to be here," "this is a lot of fun for us," and "it's our pleasure."

Follow up with a thank you card

After each gig, send a note of thanks signed by all your students. It shows gratitude and keeps the door open for future gigs.

Summary

» Gigs are a great way to hone performance, learn professionalism, and generate revenue for your program.

» Through proper planning, you will be able to set a full calendar of engagements.

» Communicate with your client to ensure they will be satisfied.

ENHANCING

CHAPTER 17

Live Sound for Pop A Cappella

by John Gentry

One of my early mentors once said to me, "A good sound engineer can make a mediocre group sound amazing, but a bad sound engineer can make a great group sound terrible."

Over the years I have found an excess of evidence to prove this statement. Whether it's the annual spring concert at your school or a performance in a 4,000-seat amphitheater, the "man behind the curtain" and the equipment he is using can make or break the sound of the group. In this chapter we will explore the equipment necessary to set up a live sound system for pop a cappella and some tips on how to properly engineer this gear to create the sound you desire. With the sentiment of the beginning quote of this chapter, I will strongly suggest that you find a dedicated sound engineer that will be with you as much as possible. Having a person who knows the group, the arrangements, and the sound that you want to achieve will be one of your biggest assets as you travel from one venue to the next. By the end of this chapter, you will at least have a working knowledge of what type of equipment to look for and a basic understanding of how to use it. Everything after that is simply just a matter of experience. (This is intended to be an overview and not an all-encompassing user manual.)

Equipment (Because Pop A Cappella Needs the Same Gear as a Rock Band!)

The Necessities

In the world of audio equipment, there are a plethora of brands. To just pull up your internet browser and search "sound board" or "speakers" can be daunting. In this section we will address and explain the units that are absolutely necessary, followed by some equipment that you can add on later once more experience is gained.

Microphones

This is where everything starts, the source of the sound: your mouth! Finding the right microphone is really a process of deciding how much you can spend. The industry standard, the Shure SM-58, has been used for decades in all genres of music. It is known for its durability and consistency. The Shure SM-58 microphone is certainly a cost-effective place to start. You can virtually run over it with a car and it will still work. This microphone will be familiar to nearly every sound engineer and therefore a consistent tone can be achieved from one venue to the next. One step above that would be a Shure Beta-58. It will have a better tone and give you a stronger sound than the standard SM-58. Equivalents of these models in a different brand would be the Sennheiser 835 and 845 respectively. An upgraded choice of microphone would be a Sennheiser 935 or 945. These more expensive models will improve the vocal sound in a significant way. There are also wireless counterparts to these same microphone models that will allow you to have a cleaner stage and more easily add choreography.

All of the microphones I have mentioned are of the handheld variety and should be used in a situation where each individual singer has their own mic. But what should you do if you have a large group and want to use zone mics? For a zone microphone set-up (where there are a few microphones in front picking up the whole group) you will need a different type of microphone. What we are talking about here are condenser microphones, which are much more sensitive than the handhelds we discussed in the previous paragraph. A couple of condenser microphones that are used in a cappella are the AKG C414XL and the Rode NT1A. You can put these microphones in front of each voice part, if your group stands in sections, or space them evenly across the front of the group, a few feet away. This is a positive way for a large group to get a good balance and have a natural sound. The negative side of this set-up is what's called the *proximity effect* (what happens to the sound as the source gets farther away from the microphone). As you add more space between the voice and the microphone, the fidelity of sound and the bass response decrease significantly. Many large groups create a nice sound by using zone microphones and then supplementing the solo, vocal percussion, and bass with handheld mics.

Specific to large a cappella groups, the standard zone mic set up for festivals such as ICHSA and ICCA is to set up one pair of condenser mics in the center and use handhelds to supplement. This is a good catch-all for a festival setting; however, this might not be the best option for your group depending on size, standing arrangement, and choreography. You can add another pair of small diaphragm pencil condensers, such as the AKG C1000s, raised up on a stand and pointing down at the back row of singers. If you have enough handhelds to go around, you can also share one handheld between every two singers. This will cut down slightly on the proximity effect and help with the fidelity of sound with some groups. At the end of the day, don't be afraid to delve into some trial and error with your group at rehearsal. There is one truth about how to mic an a cappella group, and that is there is no truth, only what you have found works best for your group.

Mixing Console

Also called a mixing board or sound board, this piece is the brains of the operation. Every microphone on the stage will be connected into this unit and subsequently connected to the speakers as well. The mixing console controls everything from the volume of each individual microphone to the tone of the voice coming through that microphone. This tone control is called equalization, or EQ for short. Later in the chapter we will discuss some techniques for getting the right tone out of each voice. The first thing to consider when purchasing a sound board is how many channels are needed for your group. If you have 16 kids singing, each on their own microphone, you need a mixing console with at least 16 channels. I would recommend getting a console with more channels than you need to allow for growth. You will also find yourself needing extra channels, possibly for an iPod, extra microphones for a live recording, a talkback mic for the sound engineer, etc. Just because you have enough inputs for your number of singers doesn't mean that you won't have other things you will need to hook into the console.

The next concern is what brand to look for and how much to spend. When considering the market of affordable mixing consoles, I'm not overly partial to any one brand, but with vocals you need to make sure you have as much tone control as possible.

Warning: The following statement may not make sense until later in the chapter, but trust me on this one . . . Ask your sales rep to only show you mixing consoles that have Dual Parametric Mid-Range EQ. Even if you don't understand exactly what that means now, you will come to know why that is a hugely important feature for a cappella sound. You should expect to spend around $1,000 for a decent mixing console for 16 channels or higher. In most cases, there is a reason why some mixing consoles are sold inexpensively—to some extent, you get what you pay for.

31-Band Graphic Equalizer

Sit tight! The explanation of this unit will be a bit technical, but I believe this to be a crucial part of the sound system, even if the engineer is not totally comfortable with its operation. There are two main purposes for this unit: controlling the tone of the overall sound and controlling any feedback in the room. We spoke a bit about controlling the tone of each individual voice with the mixing console, but some overall correction is needed as well to compensate for acoustic deficiencies in the room. Every microphone plugged into the mixing console should subsequently be sent through the 31-Band Graphic EQ so that any tone changes that need to be made to the overall sound can be adjusted on this unit. We will talk more specifically in a later section about getting the tone you want for the venue in which you are performing.

Another function of the 31-Band Graphic EQ is to help solve the issue of feedback, that high-pitched squeal or low rumble that seems to pop up out of thin air. Everyone has heard that sound at a concert or a speaking engagement, often when someone turns on a really loud microphone or gets too close to a speaker, but what is actually causing this spike of sound? The technical explanation of feedback is when a certain frequency is so loud that it creates a "squeal" in the speakers, which subsequently re-enters a microphone, which subsequently is sent back out of the speakers, which subsequently re-enters . . . you get the idea—it is a vicious loop of sound! A 31-Band Graphic EQ will help suppress this problem by removing some of the frequency that is causing the feedback loop. The only trick in this is being able to find the frequency at which the feedback is occurring. As with the previous paragraph, we will discuss the details of how to find those frequencies in a later section of this chapter.

Snake

This is not an animal to be afraid of, but a long bundled cable that will serve as the communication between the stage and the mixing console! About the size of a garden hose, the snake allows you to sit the console back in the room so you can hear what the audience hears. Think of the snake as a really long extension cord. The other alternative is to sit up near the stage and just take a random guess at what you think the rest of the room is hearing . . . this is NOT recommended! On one end of the snake is a box into which microphones can be connected and on the opposite end you will find cables to plug into the sound board. Everything on a snake is nicely labeled by number for easy organization.

Speakers

The speakers are the end of the equipment chain. Generally speaking, there are two classifications of speakers: powered and unpowered. Any speaker has to be powered by an amplifier in order to produce sound. Powered speakers will have the amplifier built-in, which means everything is packed into the same cabinet. This is a very convenient set up for groups that have frequent gigs and will be setting up and tearing down often. Unpowered speakers do not have the amplifier built-in and therefore a separate amplifier must be purchased. The unpowered set up would be recommended for a permanent set up or a larger venue where a lot of power is necessary.

Sub-woofers

A sub-woofer can be added to a regular speaker setup to enhance the low end for the bass singer and the kick drum of the vocal percussionist. A sub-woofer is a speaker that is specially designed to handle low frequencies more efficiently than a regular speaker. The same classification of powered and unpowered applies to sub-woofers as well. In order to add a sub to your speaker set up you will need to use a unit called a crossover. We will discuss the details of this unit later in this section.

Monitors

These are speakers that are on stage facing the singers so they can hear themselves. It's surprising how little you can hear on stage behind the main speakers if there are no stage monitors. Therefore, monitors are crucial to things like blend and tuning. Certain specifications can be important for a cappella monitors. Having a two-inch or greater voice coil will give you a more "in your face" sound and help you to hear the full range of the human voice. A smaller voice coil cannot usually handle the harmonics produced by an all vocal group well and can distort easily. As with main speakers, powered and unpowered models are available for stage monitors. The monitors will be controlled separately from the main speakers so the singers are able to hear their own mix without being affected by the adjustments being made for the audience. We'll talk more about the specifics of how this happens in the following section.

The Extras (Things You Don't Need Right Away, But Can Be Fun!)

Compressors

A compressor is a unit that will keep soft sounds from being too soft and prevent loud sounds from becoming overbearing. When set correctly, a compressor can even out those loud solo notes that can pop out of a phrase, as well as keep high notes in a singer's head voice from being too soft. Compressing each voice is not an absolute necessity to getting decent sound for a cappella, but when used can have a significant impact on the overall cleanliness of sound being projected through the speakers.

Effects

The two effects we will address here are reverb and delay. Both of these are commonly controlled at the mixing console. Simply stated, reverb will add some extra ambiance to the sound and delay is more of an echo of the sound. These two effects can be added to all voices or each voice individually to taste. A good starting point is to put some reverb on the vocal percussion and a small amount of delay on the soloist. Many mid-grade mixing consoles now have an effects section built directly into the console itself. Many of these built-in effects are quite usable and will add positively to your group's sound. A separate effects unit can also be hooked into the mixing console. There are many other types of effects used by pop a cappella groups which are controlled on the stage and are discussed in depth in another chapter.

Crossover

A crossover is only necessary when adding a sub-woofer to the speaker setup. The function of this unit is to split the overall sound into high frequencies and low frequencies. The low sounds are sent to the sub-woofer and the high sounds to the regular speakers. This separation takes the workload of the low frequencies away from the regular speakers and sends them to the sub-woofer, which is designed to process the low frequencies efficiently.

Cables: 'Cause You Gotta Plug This Stuff In!

XLR

These are more commonly referred to as microphone cables and the ends have three prongs. XLR cables will be used to plug microphones into the snake. Some of the other units we mentioned earlier are also connected by this type of cable.

Quarter-inch

These cables have one straight prong on the end and are used for a variety of applications. There are two types of quarter-inch cables: instrument cables and speaker cables. They both look exactly the same on the ends, so what is the difference? An instrument cable is shielded to block out any audio interference and is used just to transfer the signal of an instrument. A speaker cable has different internal construction and is made to handle the current that will be sent through

it from the amplifier to the speaker. DO NOT interchange instrument cables and speaker cables! Even though they look the same externally, you can and *will* damage your amplifier by using the wrong cable. This consideration is only applicable if using unpowered speakers. Since the amplifier is built-in to powered speakers, specific speaker cable is not necessary.

speakON®

This type of connector is specific to speaker cables as an alternative to the traditional quarter-inch end. An issue that can arise with quarter inch cables is that they can easily be pulled out of the plug if accidently pulled or stepped on by a performer. If this happens, it means no sound out front! A speakON connector goes into the jack, then twists and locks into place, thus holding the cable in place even when pulled. These connectors have a release that must be engaged before untwisting and removing the cable, similar to the idea of a prescription medicine container. Speak-on connectors should be used whenever possible to prevent any accidental loss of sound.

A note on cables: With all these different pieces of gear and types of cables, how do you know what you need? Well, you have to do your research in advance. Before you buy a mixing console, 31-Band Graphic EQ, snake, etc. you need to read the specs sheet and find out what type of cable each unit will accept. If you do your homework, you won't be left stranded at a concert with no sound because you didn't have the correct cables to plug in your gear.

Setting Up:
So You Have a Bunch of Stuff—What Do You Do With It?

How To Hook the Equipment Together

The best illustration to aid in understanding how to plug in your equipment is to *follow the signal path* through every cable and piece of gear, just as a plumber would connect pipes to route water to and from the appropriate fixtures. If you know where the sound begins and ends, it is easy to trace the path in between. You may not have realized it, but I have already walked you through the entire signal path earlier in this chapter. In the **Necessities** section, the equipment was listed in order from the beginning to the end of the signal path. If you go step by step through that list while setting up, you will have successfully completed the entire chain of equipment and cables to get sound out of the system. Most mixing consoles will have some sample signal paths illustrated in the user manual for you to visually follow, but here is a list of each necessary piece of gear and what cables you may need to hook it up:

Signal Path for Powered Speakers

Microphone → XLR → Input on Snake Box on Stage (1, 2, 3, etc.)
Other End of Snake (1, 2, 3,etc.) → Individual Channels on Mixing Console
Main Output of Mixing Console (Left/Right) → XLR → 31-Band Graphic EQ
Output of 31-Band Graphic EQ → Snake Returns (A, B, C, etc.)
Snake Box on Stage (A, B, C, etc.) → XLR → Input of Powered Speakers

Signal Path for Powered Monitors

An auxiliary output of the sound board is used as a mix separate from what the audience hears from the main speakers.

Auxiliary Output of Mixing Console → Snake Return (A, B, C, etc.)
Snake Box on Stage (A, B, C, etc.) → Input of 31-Band Graphic EQ
Output of Graphic EQ → XLR → Input of Powered Monitors

Signal Path for Unpowered Speakers

The only part of the path that changes from the above schematic when using unpowered speakers is after the snake returns to the snake box on stage. Instead of going straight from the snake return (A, B, C, etc.) to the speaker, you will go into an amplifier first, then out of the amplifier into the speaker.

Snake Box on Stage (A, B, C, etc.) → Input of Amplifier
Output of Amplifier → Speaker Cable (¼" or speakON) → Input of Unpowered Speakers

Signal Path for Unpowered Monitors

The same change discussed above is also applicable to unpowered monitors also.

Snake Box on Stage (A, B, C, etc.) → Input of 31-Band Graphic EQ
Output of Graphic EQ → XLR → Input of Amplifier
Output of Amplifier → Speaker Cable (¼" or speakON) → Input of Powered Monitors

Now, take a breath and remember, just follow the water through the pipes from beginning to end and you can't go wrong. But what if you still can't get sound to come out?

Troubleshooting

Trust your meters: The mixing console, 31-Band Graphic EQs, and amplifiers have meters that will light up when sound is being sent through them. If you see the meters lighting up on one of these units, you know the problem is after this unit in the signal path. If you are trying to send sound through a unit and no lights are lighting up, first things first: is it plugged in and powered on? Do yourself a favor and always check for power first! It saves that embarrassing explanation a half hour later when someone asks, "What was wrong?" to which you reply, "It wasn't turned on." If the unit is on, then make sure the cables are plugged into the correct output of the previous unit and into the correct input of the unit that is getting no signal. If this doesn't solve the problem, you may have a bad cable and you should swap the cable in question out with a newer one.

Getting the Sound You Want: Making the Sound System Sound Natural

How to Tune the Room and Why It Will Help

Just because you spend a decent chunk of cash buying all of this gear doesn't mean that you can turn it on and expect it to sound like Rockapella or Sonos. Every set of speakers and every venue will have acoustic deficiencies that need to be remedied. This is where tuning the room comes into play. Tuning the room is centered on the 31-Band Graphic EQ. As discussed earlier, this unit will help the overall tone of the sound and also reduce the potential for feedback, but how do you do it?

The iPod Method

I call it this because you will plug your mp3 player into the sound board and play some of your favorite professionally recorded a cappella songs through the sound system. It should be a song with a full range of frequencies and one that you are quite familiar with. Make sure you have a song with solid bass, one with a lot of different high end sounds, and try a ballad as well. Once you select a few songs for your playlist, keep it the same! Think of it as part of the scientific process—the songs will be the constant and the room/venue will be the variable for which you will need to account. The general idea is if the song sounds like it has too much bass, pull down the bass frequencies on the Graphic EQ. If the song sounds too bright, pull down the high frequencies on the Graphic EQ. If the sound is muffled or sounds nasally, then pull down the lower mid-range and higher mid-range frequencies respectively. The more experience you gain at tuning a room, the more precise and accurate you will be in selecting the correct frequencies to pull down to make that song really sound great in the venue in which you are setting up. At first, you may find yourself making general large adjustments, but as the years go by you will be working with one frequency at a time. When beginning this process, you should set the 31-Band Graphic EQ to 0 or neutral and adjust from there.

The Feedback Method

The point of this process is to intentionally create feedback and isolate the frequencies that are producing the feedback in order to pull down the specific pitch that is "squealing." To begin this process, have all of your singers stand on stage holding their microphones and turn everything on. Begin by slowly turning up the master volume on the mixing console until you begin to hear that rumble or squeal. If it is a high pitched sound, pull down the high frequencies on the 31-Band Graphic EQ until you can turn up the master volume without any feedback occurring. When beginning this process, set the 31-Band Graphic EQ to 0 or neutral and adjust from there. In practice, some combination of these two methods can and should be used to compensate for all of the deficiencies in the acoustic environment of the venue. Ninety percent of the time, I use the iPod method and then as the microphones get turned up, I find a couple more frequencies that are feeding back slightly.

Why Tune the Room?

Every room has different sonic characteristics and they are not always ideal for amplified sound. The shape, size, and materials used in the room (carpet, concrete, wood, etc.) will all have an effect on the frequencies that are emphasized.

Are you sitting down? Get up and walk to the bathroom. Yes, I'm serious. Actually get up and walk over there. Sing a major scale from the bottom of your range to the top. Did you hear a note or two that seemed louder than the others? Those notes are the frequencies that are emphasized based on the reverberation created by the hard tile surfaces, shape, and size of that particular room. If you didn't hear any notes pop out noticeably, try it again and listen closely. It may be subtle, but you will most likely hear some unevenness in the frequency response of the room.

Okay, now you can go back to your comfortable reading chair . . .

Frequencies: How Do You Know Which Ones You Are Hearing?

As was stated in earlier sections, when it comes to using a Graphic Equalizer, accuracy is gained through experience, but isn't there a way to find a starting point? Of course! All of us musicians have heard of tuning instruments to A-440, but in the world of sound engineering, we get to use that term in a totally different way. As a reminder, the specific pitch that is being referred to is the A above middle C on a piano. This particular pitch is the frequency of 440 hertz, which is the measurement unit of "cycles per second." If you look at a 31-Band Graphic EQ, one of the frequencies listed is 440, the A above middle C! The easiest way to find your way to the other frequencies is to understand what creates an octave interval. Scientifically speaking, an octave is what happens when the number of cycles per second, or hertz, is multiplied or divided by two. For example, the frequency of the A below middle C would be 220Hz (440/2) and the frequency of the A one octave above A-440 would be 880Hz (440x2). This should get you started on identifying which frequencies are being

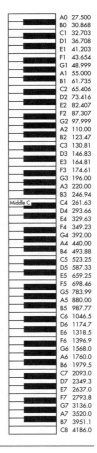

Note	Frequency
A0	27.500
B0	30.868
C1	32.703
D1	36.708
E1	41.203
F1	43.654
G1	48.999
A1	55.000
B1	61.735
C2	65.406
D2	73.416
E2	82.407
F2	87.307
G2	97.999
A2	110.00
B2	123.47
C3	130.81
D3	146.83
E3	164.81
F3	174.61
G3	196.00
A3	220.00
B3	246.94
C4 (Middle C)	261.63
D4	293.66
E4	329.63
F4	349.23
G4	392.00
A4	440.00
B4	493.88
C5	523.25
D5	587.33
E5	659.25
F5	698.46
G5	783.99
A5	880.00
B5	987.77
C6	1046.5
D6	1174.7
E6	1318.5
F6	1396.9
G6	1568.0
A6	1760.0
B6	1979.5
C7	2093.0
D7	2349.3
E7	2637.0
F7	2793.8
G7	3136.0
A7	3520.0
B7	3951.1
C8	4186.0

created in a feedback loop or which notes are too "boomy" or resonant in the venue (or in your bathroom as exampled earlier).

Now that the sound system is tuned to sound great in the room, we need to move on to individual voices.

Sound Check

Before I formally start the explanation of the sound check process, we need to cover one huge no-brainer that is all too often overlooked and can be a huge time waster. Go buy some white artists tape and a permanent marker, and then label the channels on the board! Simply write the name of the singer or the voice part they are singing under each channel. I have been a part of too many sound checks where things sound less than excellent and after a half hour of wasted time, it turns out the sound engineer did not know who was in what channel.

Okay, now that we have covered the no-brainer, we can discuss the specifics of the sound check, which is the process of going through each individual voice or microphone, setting the correct volume levels and getting the tone adjusted. It is important to go through this process one microphone at a time to make sure each one is working properly and that you're getting the best sound from each singer. Much of the knowledge of frequencies and pitch detailed in the previous section can also be applied to each individual voice.

Remember the confusing reference to dual parametric mid-range EQ that I made when explaining the mixing console? Now we are going to explore what that means and why it is imperative to working with a cappella groups.

Begin sound check by having *one* of your kids sing through a piece of a song. On that channel of the mixing console, you will start by setting the gain level. The gain adjustment sets the overall sensitivity of that channel. A good starting point is to set the gain so that the meter on that channel hits right at 0, or called in some cases "unity." If your console does not have a meter for every channel, hit the "solo" or "pfl" button and this will make the main meters on the console function for that particular channel. This "unity" gain is simply a starting point and can be adjusted up or down as you bring the fader up for volume and as you try to get the blend of the whole group.

Next, you will be adjusting the tone of that one voice. The beauty of a parametric EQ is that it allows you to select which frequency you want to adjust. So if a voice sounds muffled you should pull down some of the low mid-range frequencies. If a voice sounds "honky" or "nasally" you should find a higher mid-range frequency to pull down. Repeat for each voice until the whole group has been individually sound checked. *Do yourself a favor and don't skip this step!* Many groups just turn on all the microphones at once and say, "Go for it!" Even the most experienced a cappella sound engineer may have trouble picking out frequencies in an individual voice if everyone is singing together.

Subtractive vs. Additive EQ

In a previous section, **Getting the Sound You Want**, you have already read the phrase "pull down the frequency" a total of eight times. I apologize for the redundancy, but there is a point to my overuse of the phrase. Generally speaking, *always subtract frequencies from the mix to adjust the tone as opposed to adding frequencies.* If you think of the mix as a physical space, you need to create room for all of the sound to co-exist happily. If you keep adding more and more sound by boosting frequencies instead of pulling them down, you will quickly run out of space in this figurative room. It's like trying to fill a five-gallon bucket with ten gallons of water—it will always end up messy.

Effects

We discussed some general ideas about effects earlier; here we will get a little more specific. For an outboard effects unit, you can find a schematic in the manual of your effects unit on how to properly wire this unit to your console. After it is all hooked up, you will be able to add these effects to each voice individually using an auxiliary send. This adjustment will be in the same place as your auxiliary sends for your monitor mixes. If your console has built in effects, there should be an auxiliary labeled specifically as effects. There are several different types of reverbs that are created to mimic different types of rooms and venues. You don't need reverb on every single voice, just a little light reverb on some of the voices to create a nice depth and character to the overall sound of the group. I usually add reverb to some of the higher voice parts and don't add any to the bass singers unless the song calls for that specific effect. I like to use a vocal plate to add a nice sparkle to the sound.

Delay, unlike reverb, is an echo of the sound. Delay is great as long as it is used in a musical way. Adding delay to a soloist on some songs will add extra character to the voice without making it sound like it's in a cave as reverb can sometimes do. A fun artistic use for delay is to add it to just the last chord or two of a song that has an abrupt ending. This will create that echo effect that can be heard on the end of many recorded a cappella songs.

The main goal of adding effects is simply to know what you are looking for in the sound. If you know the original song has some significant delay, try it in rehearsal till you get it right. If an original tune has an extremely ambient character, try adding different types of reverb to different voices until you achieve the goal at hand.

Getting the Group to Sound Great Together: Scooping Out Space in the Mix

The idea of subtractive EQ is crucial in getting all of the voices to sound good as an ensemble. If one voice has a little too much of any certain frequency you may not notice it while they are singing alone. However, if another voice or two is also producing a little too much of that same frequency, pretty soon the overall mix of the group will have an excess of that frequency. Imagine being in a room with someone that used a little too much cologne that day. It might be annoying but manageable. Now picture yourself in a room with three or four people that went overboard on the fragrance—it will quickly become unbearable. This is a common problem when setting the EQ for each voice in an a cappella group. The mix can easily become uncomfortably bright or unintelligibly muffled if too many voices are too heavy in a certain frequency. To counteract this issue, you should be conscious of "scooping out" frequencies in certain voices. For example, if the bass is strong in a certain frequency range, subtract those frequencies in the other male voices. The end result of this process may leave an individual voice sounding thin or affected, but in the scheme of the entire mix, it will produce the best overall tone.

Vocal Percussion: The Exception to the Rule

When setting the EQ for vocal percussion, there will still be some mid-range frequencies that need to be subtracted. However, to make these sounds truly emulate the sound of a real drum set, it is often necessary to add some low and high frequencies to the sound. In most groups, the percussion doesn't pop through in the mix properly if these frequencies are not added. A nice plate or hall reverb is also helpful to add to vocal percussion to replicate the natural resonance of acoustic drums.

Running the Show: Set It and Forget It or Keep Making Adjustments?

Active vs. Passive Mixing

There are two schools of thought with respect to what a sound engineer should do during the performance. The idea of passive mixing still embodies all of the techniques addressed in setting up and sound checking but does not include many changes during the show. This is the "set it and forget it" approach and this leaves all of the work up to the performers to achieve the best blend. While I do believe in promoting proper microphone technique and training your singers to listen for their own blend, a passive audio mixer will most likely leave your group with a stagnant sound that gets boring halfway through the first song. An active audio engineer should be involved in the music as much as the performers on stage. If the person behind the sound board is constantly keeping an ear out and adjusting for the correct balance and blend, your group will come across as trained professionals! This is the perfect opportunity to again plug the importance of having a dedicated sound engineer for your group. This engineer should preferably be someone with enough musical knowledge and/or training to understand blend and balance, but even just consistently having someone there with you at every rehearsal and show will be a huge step in the right direction of achieving an active mix from your engineer.

Catching the Solos

This part is simple! Have someone from your group write down the set list and notate which person/microphone channel on the mixing console has solos and duets during each song. There is nothing that will take the audience out of the groove more quickly than missing the first sentence of a solo because the sound engineer is trying to track down which microphone to turn up. The only issue with turning up a soloist is EQ—if a voice is set to blend in with the entire group, it may sound thin or bright as a soloist. A quick fix for this is to add back a little bit of the mid-range frequencies during the solo that were previously subtracted to create a group blend.

Hopefully you now have a basic knowledge of the equipment and the techniques necessary to create a great a cappella sound for a live show. If you feel overwhelmed by this chapter, take a moment and then read it again. Many people have become decent sound engineers through the simple process of trial and error. You are already one step ahead after being armed with the knowledge and specific a cappella advice in this chapter. Whether you take a crack at being a sound engineer yourself, hire a professional, or mentor an interested student, remember that the engineer is as much a performer as those on stage. The only difference is that nobody sees the sound engineer. In practice, the director of the group should be freed to do their job fully. Knowing how the sound system works and understanding the process will help any director immensely in his or her job, but separation of duties is most always the best practice. Let the director direct, let the singers sing, and let the sound engineer . . . well, engineer the sound. When these individual roles are perfected and begin to work as one cohesive unit, the sky is the limit!

SUMMARY

» While you need to understand sound basics, get a board operator as often as possible.

» Swap group members to run sound if needed and when practical.

» Assign group members specific sound set-up and tear-down jobs.

CHAPTER 18

Microphone Technique

Although mastery of microphone technique is an art unto itself, and quite personal (making the microphone an extension of your voice), there are a few simple guidelines that will help you get started. These presume the use of a handheld microphone, a Shure SM-58 or the like. With this type of microphone, the singer has personal control at all times. With zone microphones, the only control the singer has is where they are positioned in relation to the mic stand.

The Components

The microphone is comprised of three main parts: the body, capsule, and head. If you imagine the microphone as an ice cream cone, the body would be the cone. The head is the ice cream sitting on top. The capsule is contained inside the head, and is the part of the microphone that actually picks up sound through the use of the microphone's diaphragm, a flat surface that works much like your eardrum. Attached to that surface is a small induction coil. When sound strikes the diaphragm, it causes the induction coil to vibrate within a magnetic field. Those vibrations are translated into a signal that eventually is processed into sound.

The head is there to protect the capsule and also contains a small bit of mesh that is known as a "pop filter." This helps limit the amount of noise that is created by your breath as you sing into the microphone. Without a pop filter, explosive constants (like p and t) can create very loud spikes in the signal.

How To Hold the Microphone

Generally speaking, you should only hold the microphone by the body. Do not let your hand touch the head of the microphone. Because the head surrounds the capsule for protection, blocking it with your hand sets up a mini "echo chamber" for sound. It can cause your tone to distort or sound muffled. Sometimes "cupping" the mic head in your hand will create a sound that is good for specific vocal percussion noises or intentionally distorted tones like that of a guitar, but for most singing it is best to not cup the head of the mic.

Most handheld microphones use a cardioid/unidirectional pickup pattern, which means that they pick up the most sound in front of the head, and some additional sound from the sides. This helps eliminate the possibility of feedback from picking up anything but the primary sound source (your voice). To that end, you must sing directly into the microphone. Imagine that the microphone is a flashlight. You should sing with the microphone in a position so that the flashlight's beam would shine directly into your open mouth. Many new singers will hold the microphone straight up and down, as if they were about to lick an ice-cream cone. This leads to singing across the top of the microphone, which leads to a very weak signal. To test for the best position, sing a long tone and tip the microphone back and forth until it is pointed directly at your mouth, picking up the most sound possible.

What Is the Correct Distance?

The closer you hold the microphone to your mouth, the better the frequency response will be. This is specifically noticeable in the bass range. An easy way to test this proximity effect is to begin speaking with the microphone at arm's length, slowly bringing the mic head closer and closer to your mouth until it touches your lips. As it gets closer, you'll hear the fidelity of sound increase dramatically.

Most singers hold the microphone too far away from their mouths. This often happens because the singer doesn't want to sound too loud in the overall mix. This creates a negative cycle. Even if they are singing loudly, the signal coming into the sound board is not as strong as it should be. Hearing a weak signal, the sound man is likely to turn the mic level higher. The singer might try to compensate by pulling out farther. As this back-and-forth continues, the fidelity of sound suffers.

Soloists should keep the mic head very close, even touching their lips. Background singers should pull away slightly more, maybe an inch. For passages or notes that are sung very loudly, you may pull away as much as four to five inches, but no more. If the balance of voices cannot be achieved within these guidelines, then the sound board is not properly calibrated. Singers must work with the sound technician to set levels before the performance begins.

Bass Specific Tips

We discuss the bass in Chapter 13 **What About the Bass?** but here are some quick tips:

» When singing as a bass guitar, keep the microphone head on your lips. Some basses will move the mic up a bit to rest on the upper lip under the nose. This comes down to personal preference and requires some experimentation.

» When the bass is singing lyrics or in chords, they should use the mic as any other singer.

» Remember that the bass frequencies are best produced when the microphone is closest to the mouth.

» During sound check, don't forget to test the bass signal strength both as an instrument sound and as a natural voice.

» If using an octave pedal, be sure that the level of sound is consistent when the pedal is both on and off.

Vocal Percussion Specific Tips

» Many VPs will begin by holding the microphone too far away from their mouths. This is because they don't want to make the microphone "pop" with air. That, however, is the very function of vocal percussion—to make percussive, punchy noises. Make sure you have the microphone right on your mouth, start with the microphone level low, then turn up the gain and volume until you reach a desired sound.

» Some VPs will "cup" the microphone, wrapping their hand around the entire head of the mic. Then they make their beatbox sounds into the hole at the top of their hand. This funnels the sound into the diaphragm more directly and allows less air to escape the capsule, resulting in punchier drum sounds. Experiment with "cupped" and "non-cupped" techniques to create a broader palate of sounds for different musical needs.

Various Proximity Tricks

» Try singing a long note and moving the microphone in and out of the sound stream.

» Vary the distance from your mouth to create crescendi/decrescendi in both volume and tone.

» Move the microphone from side to side to create a flange effect in the voice.

How To Clean Your Microphone

The best way to clean your microphone is to remove the head (or grille). Most microphones have heads that unscrew. Make sure that you do not pull on the grille too forcefully or torque it. You don't want to damage the capsule underneath.

Once the grille is removed, it can be cleaned without damaging the microphone. Since most of what dirties the grille comes from the human body (saliva, etc.), plain water should do the trick. If you like, add a small amount of a mild dishwashing liquid to the water to act as a disinfectant and to help remove odors from the foam windscreen. If there is lipstick or other material stuck in the grille, simply use a toothbrush with soft bristles to clean it off.

The most important thing to remember is that you must allow the head/grille to completely dry before reattaching it to the microphone. Microphones don't like water! You can either air dry the grille or use a hair dryer on a low-heat setting to speed the process. Just be sure not to get the hair dryer too close to the grille, as excessive heat can melt some windscreen material.

If you do not have time to completely clean your microphones and are passing them from person to person within one rehearsal, consider using small alcohol swabs to at least swab off the outside of the grille to improve the hygiene of the microphone.

Summary

» With handheld microphones, closer proximity = better sound.

» Use proximity tricks to create interesting vocal effects.

» Basses may need two placements, one for instrument sounds and one for lyrics.

» VPs can cup the mic head to create punchier drum sounds.

» Keep your microphones clean and dry for good hygiene and long life.

CHAPTER 19

Effects (FX) Pedals

by Christopher Given Harrison

How and Why Do I Use FX Pedals?

FX pedals further the character, depth, contrast, and originality of your arrangements and performances. They are by no means a crutch, or some substitute for musicality. They are creative tools that allow one to expand upon the statement already being made with the interpretation of the music.

Let's say your group performs a piece from the era of early rock'n'roll—perhaps an Elvis song. Your lead singer will probably put on at least a hint of an Elvis impression, manipulating his or her vowels to sit in the back of the mouth, slurring certain consonants, etc. The point of this is to take the listener back to the "Sun Records" trademark sound. You know what could take them just that much further? A hint of slap-back delay on the lead (which you can hear on just about everything from that era) and a nice, round, quiet octavizer on the bass for that upright "rock-a-billy" sound.

Or you're performing something modern, such as Beyonce's "Halo." You can dial in the same long ballad-timed-delays ("far away echo" sounds that occur in time with the music) that can be heard on the studio track, as well as a little synth bass to beef up the low end of the choruses. The charisma and chops of your lead singer and the musical precision of your hard-working background vocals are still the elements that make or break the performance. The FX can be the gloss coating that allows us to depart from where we are and further immerse ourselves in the journey of the performance.

Definitions of FX Pedals

While there are (of course) many exceptions, FX pedals tend to do one or more of three specific jobs:

» Accentuation: coloring the sound to make it more distinct or interesting

» Extension: reaching beyond the natural limitations of the human voice

» Clean-up: improving the clarity or effectiveness of the sound

Examples of Accentuation Pedals

Distortion/Overdrive

Literally overloads the signal path. This can sound like anything from a broken speaker to an electric guitar solo from the glam-rock era.

Flanger/Phaser/Chorus

Takes one voice, splits it into two, gently manipulates the copy, and plays both simultaneously.

Tremolo

Quick and consistent volume fluctuation of the voice. Imagine vibrato, but rather than the pitch bending slightly up and down at high speeds, the *volume* fluxes up and down at high speeds.

Delay (short, such as "slap-back")

Makes a copy of the incoming sound and plays it back a fraction of a second later, one or more times.

If any of these or the following descriptions leave you wondering what they actually sound like, take a quick spin on YouTube. Search any of these terms and watch about five pedal demonstrations. By the fifth one, you'll get the gist of what the pedal does.

Examples of Extension Pedals

Octavizer

Duplicates the incoming voice one (or several) octave lower.

Harmonizer

Splits the incoming voice into multiple voices in intervals specified by the user.

Looper

Records a long segment of the incoming voice (four or eight bars, for example) and plays it back in a repeating loop.

Delay (long)

Like the loop station, plays back a copy of the incoming voice several seconds later, but unlike the loop station, the repeating voice dies away gradually.

Examples of Extension Pedals

EQ

Allows volume control over specific frequency ranges of the voice (like on a car's sound system).

Noise Suppression/Gate

Cuts the voice out entirely when it comes through at or below a designated level (absolutely necessary when using distortion and overdrive FX to prevent feedback).

Compression

A full explanation of this pedal's operations would be rather lengthy. In short, a compressor shrinks the distance between the sound's quietest and loudest volume levels. It can help a quiet voice cut through a loud background.

The extension pedals are slightly more inconspicuous while in action. It's easier to hear what they do when you switch them off, rather than listening for their effect while they're on.

Which Pedals Should I Get *and* Where Should I Get Them?

In general, I make a blanket recommendation of BOSS pedals to get you started. The sound quality is great, the construction is durable so they tend to last a while, they are functionally reliable (some cheaper FX units have discrepancies in the production of the effected sound), and they can be purchased rather inexpensively through second-hand channels like craigslist.org or in the used section of amazon.com. But in case you'd like specific recommendations across the board, here is a list:

Distortion

BOSS DS-1: Simple, classic, and cheap.

Overdrive

Ibanez TS9 "Tube Screamer": Classic, not as cheap.

Flanger

BOSS BF-3: Lots of variety and pretty color.

Phaser

MXR Phase 90: Simple, effective, and cheap.

Chorus

BOSS CE-5: Lots of variety, but boring color.

Tremolo

Electro-Harmonix Stereo Pulsar: Lots of control and in stereo!

Delay

MXR M169 Carbon Copy Analog Delay: Simple.
Line 6 DL4: Insanely awesome and complicated.

Octavizer

BOSS OC-2: Creates single and double octaves. Awesome, but hard to find.
EBS Octabass: Very smooth, but one octave only.

Harmonizer

Digitech Harmony Man: Can split incoming voice into two additional voices up to one octave above or below, and in a variety of ways.
Digitech Whammy: Creates one additional voice and allows for glissando and pitch bending.

Looper

Digitech Jamman Series:
    Jamman Solo: Standard "single" size, 35 minutes of recording time, and computer "sync"-able.
    Jamman Stereo: 35 minutes of recording time (or 16 hours on SD card) and computer "sync"-able.

EQ

BOSS GE-7: Simple, durable, and effective.

Noise Suppressor

BOSS NS-2: Simple, durable, and effective.

Compressor

MXR DynaComp: Simple, effective, and cheap.

To begin, I'd suggest getting an octavizer, delay, and flanger, phaser, or chorus. You can experiment with any of these without too much danger of feedback or loud blasts of sound. This is a must at the beginning of your pedal journey since the very best way to learn to fully utilize FX pedals is to play around with them for hours! The delay and flanger/phaser/ chorus you'll likely use on your lead singer, or a "guitar solo," and the octavizer you'll likely use on your most reliable and pitch-accurate bass singer. Because almost all pedals have a quarter-  inch input and the microphone you're using almost certainly has an XLR output, you'll need an impedance converter. These are usually about $15. Get a "Whirlwind Little IMP Low to High Impedance Matcher."

Here's the order of your chain:

Microphone → XLR cable → Impedance Converter → Pedal → ¼-inch Cable → Amp

Start on your own. Plug in, switch on, and just sing whatever comes to mind while fiddling with the various knobs on the pedal. Pretty quickly you'll discover settings that you don't like (or that are sonically annoying) and settings that you do like—

sounds you think are cool and that you'd like to use. Keep a notebook handy and make a note of the position of the dials when you like the way something sounds.

Once you have a collection of favorite settings, invite another set of ears that you trust to come listen to you sing through the pedal. Outsider perspective is endlessly valuable. Your inclination will likely be to push an effect a little harder than necessary so you can hear it clearly while you're singing. Your second set of ears will help you more accurately calibrate your setting. If you don't want to invite someone else to listen, record yourself and listen back. Adjust your favorite settings accordingly. By doing all this, you're establishing a good starting place for your ensemble's integration of pedal usage.

I've Mastered the Octave, Delay, and Flanger. I Want More . . .

Distortion/Overdrive

This is fantastically fun whenever covering a song with an actual electric guitar solo, especially when the singer is female. If they work at it, it'll sound almost indistinguishable from an actual electric guitar!

Note: When using any type of distortion or overdrive with a microphone, you *must* also use a noise suppressor or gate. Otherwise, you'll fill your whole world with screaming feedback.

Here's how to rig it up (using the BOSS NS-2 noise suppressor):

Microphone → XLR cable → Impedance Converter → NS-2 Input → ¼-inch Cable from NS-2 Send → Distortion Pedal Input → ¼-inch Cable from Distortion Pedal Output → NS-2 Return → ¼-inch Cable from NS-2 Output → Amp

Here's how to safely start playing to find your settings:

» On the distortion pedal, turn the knob labeled "level" or "output" all the way down (to the left).

» On the noise suppressor, turn the "mute/reduction" knob to the "mute" setting (pointing straight up to 12:00). Turn the "threshold" knob all the way up and the "decay" knob all the way down. Tap the pedal so that the little red light is off (turning it on will mute everything entirely).

» Tap the distortion pedal until the little red light is on, and then very slowly begin creeping the "output" knob to the right while you sing into the microphone.

» Once you have a quiet or manageable sound coming through, feel free to safely play with the knobs marked "drive," "tone," "color," etc. to find your desired sound. Add some long delay and go Hendrix!

Harmonizer

This can be especially useful if your ensemble is small and you'd like to thicken the inner parts, or if you're covering something modern in the electro-vein of Imogen Heap (because of its digital vocodery timbre).

Here's how to rig it up (using the Digitech Harmony Man):

Microphone → XLR cable → Impedance Converter → Harmony Man "guitar clean input" → ¼-inch Cable from Output Left (mono) → Amp

Here's how to start:

> » Set the "mix" knob to 12:00. This will give you an equal amount of fundamental tone and harmonized tones.

> » Roll both "voice" knobs (labeled "voice 1" and "voice 2") to the right until simple single digits appear. These single digits refer to the number of half-steps above or below the incoming voice that you'd like the pedal to generate new voices.

> » Start out with a major triad. Set "voice 1" to "4" and "voice 2" to "7" (four half-steps for a major third and seven half-steps for a perfect fifth).

> » Click the left pedal (harmony on/off) to make sure the effect is activated.

> » Sing through like this a while. Play with other intervallic variations.

> » When you find one you'd like to keep, tap the "store" button twice.

> » The right pedal controls which "page" you're on. There are four "pages" that you can scroll through by taping the right pedal, each with their own customizable setting (unfortunately, you can only scroll through them forward). So let's say you want your singer to be able to jump back and forth between major and minor triads. Set the voices on page one to "4" and "7," the voices on page two to "3" and "7," page three the same as page one, and page four the same as page two.

The majority of the other functions provided by this pedal rely on incoming sounds to be in concert pitch, thus making them very tricky to use in the context of a cappella because of the likelihood of drifting tonic. It can be done, of course, but it is no easy feat.

Looper

This is an absolute lifesaver for any group that can't spare their beatboxer's voice, but still needs his or her beats!

Here's how to rig it up (using the Digitech Jamman Stereo):

Microphone → XLR Cable → Jamman Stereo XLR Mic input →
¼-inch Cable from Left Mono Out → Amp

Here's how to start:

» Turn all four small knobs all the way to the left: loop level, rhythm level, mic level, and instrumental (inst.) level.

» Turn the one large knob to the right until the digital read says "20" (each one of these numbers is a separate "tape loop" upon which you can record and layer sounds). The first 13 or so are occupied with obnoxious demo loops. You can delete them later if you like.

» Sing into the mic and slowly turn the "mic level" knob to the right until you get a reasonable volume coming through the amp and the little green light just to the left of the digital read is glowing.

   • **Note:** If the green light turns yellow or red, you're overloading the signal inside the pedal and should turn your "mic level" back to the left until your loudest singing or beatboxing only turns the light green. If the sound from the amp is still too quiet, give yourself more volume from the amp.

» Once you've found your ideal "mic level," adjust the "loop level" knob to match it. For example, if the "mic level" is at about 11:00, set the "loop level" at about 11:00.

» Practice performing a simple two-bar loop a few times.

» When it feels steady, hit the lower left silver button on the downbeat of your performed loop. This is going to record your performance. When you get to the end of your loop and are about to begin again, hit the same silver button on the same downbeat. Try to think of hitting the button as part of the musical performance. The more musical you are in your operation of the looper pedal, the closer to perfect the loop length will be.

   • So it goes: (button! - 2 - 3 - 4 - 1 - 2 - 3 - 4 - button!).

» The pedal will go straight from recording your loop to playing it back in time. If the loop is imperfect or you'd like to try again, click the lower right silver button to stop the loop.

» The quickest way to delete what you've recorded is to turn the larger knob one click to left, then one click back to the right again.

» Once you've recorded a loop that is to your liking, you can layer on top of it by clicking the lower left silver knob again while the loop is still playing, putting the pedal in "overdub" mode.

» To review, the lower left silver button functions are:

   • First click = record.

   • Second click = playback.

   • Third click = overdub.

- All of the following clicks will toggle back and forth between playback and overdub.

» If you'd like to save your loop, slowly push the "store" button twice. Your loop will remain on that "page" (we'll call the glowing numbers on the digital read "pages") until you delete it.

» You can delete your loop by slowly pressing the "delete" button twice.

Multi-FX Pedal

If you love any or all of the single FX pedals you've explored thus far and are certain you'd like a great many more, you can save a lot of money and physical space by going with a multi-FX pedal (my personal favorite at the moment is the Line 6: M9). A multi-FX pedal contains digital emulations of sometimes hundreds of classic FX pedals. The possible combinations are endless! If you've understood and successfully navigated your pedal experience thus far, you'll explore multi-FX pedals with ease.

Summary

» *Always* use a noise suppressor or gate with distortion/overdrive pedals.

» When stringing together a series of pedals that include a delay pedal, it is best to put the delay pedal at the end of the chain. When a delay pedal is placed before certain FX pedals (especially an octavizer or harmonizer), it can hinder their ability to function.

» When initially exploring the delay pedal, be careful not to turn the knob labeled "feedback" or "repeat" too far to the right. This is the one situation in which you can accidentally generate loud feedback with a delay pedal.

» Some octavizers create an unwanted "scary" sound in the higher frequencies. An EQ pedal can be used to remove (or at least reduce) the presence of these sounds by pulling the higher frequency bands down. Place the EQ pedal after the octavizer in your pedal chain.

» Some octavizers tend to track certain vowels better than others. If your octavizer is glitching at all, experiment with different vowels until you find one that causes the pedal to glitch the least. In the sections of arrangements where you plan to use the octave pedal, change all vowels to the one you find works best with the pedal (this applies only to the pedal user, of course).

GROWING

CHAPTER 20

A Cappella Meets PR:
Publicize, Fundraise, Recruit, and Inspire

In this chapter, we'll look at a few ways to use your a cappella group to generate public interest in your program. Of course, these ideas aren't genre-specific, but the smaller size of a cappella groups, as well as the lack of props, back-up band, and heavy choreography, allow them to do things other groups just can't do. Plus, your a cappella group is singing music that is accessible to the general public.

National Anthem / Halftime Performances
It goes without saying that sports are kind of a big deal in our culture. It doesn't hurt the band department to have tie-ins, such as marching band with football, pep band with basketball, etc. How can you get in on this action? How can you reach the "mainstream" crowd that attends the games?

Singing the National Anthem is the easiest way! Athletic boosters are always calling us to sing "The Star-Spangled Banner." If they haven't called you yet, *offer*. Remember that the National Anthem you sing doesn't have to be a difficult arrangement. You can start by singing just the melody, or even easy harmony in some sections, if that's all your group can manage. We've done everything from unison singing to Derric Johnson's 8-part masterpiece (as sung by Disney's Voices of Liberty). In fact, that 8-part version was "tradition" for years until I decided it was just too much work for an event that has horrible microphones (if any), and where the applause will cut off the end of the song. That's the beauty of it—you don't even have to be stellar. Just sing well and then: let's play ball! Singing the National Anthem just builds good will.

If you want to go one step further, set up some sound equipment and sing a few tunes at halftime. Of course, you'll have to work things out with the athletic director *and* the band director, if they're scheduled to play, but it can be a great thing. Once a year, our school has a football game against a school that won't bring their marching band. During that game, we sing three songs at halftime after our marching band plays. The crowd loves it!

Singing Valentines

If you're looking for a great way to raise your profile and earn a little extra cash for your group, try Singing Valentines. They are a great combination of publicity and fundraising, as well as being universally popular. I've done them with my college quartet, as an adult with my barbershop chorus, and for ten years with my high school groups. They are great fun and have the added benefit of requiring no up-front investment.

We'll divide Singing Valentines into five stages: planning, promotion, sales, performances, and wrap-up.

Planning

» *Get permission.* Well . . . if you have to, that is. As a high school group, we have to ask the principal. College groups might need to file with their activities office.

» *Figure out numbers in advance: how many can you do?* Take the time to realistically plan your capacity, taking travel time into account. There's nothing more embarrassing than overselling and going back to the buyer with nothing but an apology. This might mean a few less dollars for you, but this could be the buyer's only romantic gesture!

» *If you have a large group, consider dividing up into quartets.* It's fun to sing together, but more groups means more money. You are doing this for money, right?

» *Have a song for guys and a song for girls.* Clearly post this! It seems obvious, but many people are embarrassed to ask and thus will not order. Alternately, you can use songs that are gender neutral, such as "Stand By Me."

Promotion

» *Go on the radio.* We sing on our student station and morning announcements. Colleges have their own stations. Your local stations may be open to helping as well.

» *Put up posters:* Who, what, when, where, and why.

» *Sales table.* We sell at lunch in the cafeteria, often singing around the table or playing one of our CDs. You could also sell at concerts.

Sales

» *Let people know where the money goes.* It doesn't hurt to promote this as a good cause, as well as a fun event.

» *Have upgrades available.* Flowers, chocolates . . . even your CD as a keepsake of the serenade! Upgrades offer more chances to make money, and many people will gladly let you become their one-stop Valentine shop.

» *Get tons of information.* Don't just get the time and place of the serenade. Make sure you have the buyers' cell phone numbers in case something goes wrong. And find out from the buyer if there's something you can reference that would make the serenade especially meaningful or entertaining.

Performances

» *Announce yourselves and find the "victim."*

» *Play to the audience while you serenade.* Don't forget that you are not only serenading someone, you are selling your group! Because this performance will only be one or two songs, explode with energy! Think in advance of things you can do to get the onlookers excited. Have several members of the group "fight" over the person, or surround them as you sing until you are uncomfortably close.

» *Take business cards with you.* It's always a good time to promote!

» *Thank everyone and announce yourselves again as you leave.*

Wrap-up

» *As with everything you do as a group, take notes of what went well and what could be improved.*

» *Circle back and thank everyone involved (your principal, radio station, etc).*

With a little forethought, you can really make Singing Valentines a hit for your group. If you do them annually, you can expect to get "regulars" and watch your sales grow. You don't have to stop with Valentines, either. You can run similar programs around prom time ("Ask her to prom with a song!"), Sweetest Day, or Christmas. No matter what you do, have a good time. Everyone loves a serenade!

Have Microphones, Will Travel . . . Literally!
(Or *How to Sing on a Parade Float*)

This is the story of how our a cappella group ended up rolling down Main Street on a parade float, singing on our PA system with a portable generator.

As we mentioned earlier in this chapter, the choir department doesn't have automatic tie-ins to mass culture like the band department. Marching bands are often staples of local holiday parades. Why should they have all the fun? If you can find a truck to pull a flatbed trailer (preferably with side rails, or you'll need to build some), you can sing your way into the hearts of thousands of parade watchers! You can set up your sound gear on the flatbed and power it with a small portable gasoline generator.

I can't recommend this more highly. What a treat to hear a cappella coming down the street on a PA system. The crowd eats it up, and your group will get tons of exposure. You can even have friends of the group hand out CD order forms or fliers advertising your next concert.

Benefits of the Float:

» Publicity for your program

» Opportunity to hand out fliers for concerts or CD sales

» FUN for the kids

» Recruiting for your program

» Generating future gigs (community clubs like Rotary and Lion's Club will all have members at the parade)

Things to Remember:

» *Make sure you have a rain plan.* In fact, have it ready even if it isn't supposed to rain. One year, *sprinklers* went off near our float and our gear got wet. Keep trash bags and tarps at the ready.

» *You will need a generator for power.* You can rent them easily enough. We put ours in the bed of the pickup, not on the float. The PA system will drown out the motor noise, but your singers will need to hear the monitors (and that generator gets hot).

» *Test everything in advance.* That includes riding around with your singers. The first time we did this, we learned the hard way that we needed sturdier hand rails (no one was hurt . . . it was funny). Doing a dry run in a parking lot will keep everyone safe on parade day and allow you to set the PA levels. You won't be able to get much of a read as you are running the sound board from the truck as the parade moves along.

After our first float appearance, we immediately heard, "You're doing that again next year, right?" This year marked our third go-round and we will keep the tradition going. Not only do we gain exposure from the parade route, we have now become part of the entertainment at the nearby craft festival. After the parade is over, we just drive straight to the gig and park—the float is an instant stage.

There are lots of festivals, so get out there and give it a go. The hardest part is doing the constant "princess wave" to the crowd while you sing.

"Your-School-Name-Here" Idol

I can remember long ago thinking, "How great would it be if, instead of *Monday Night Football,* there was *Monday Night Choir?*" Well, that wish came true, in a sense, with the arrival of *American Idol*. *Idol* has been around now for ten seasons, and earns the highest ratings in all of television. In fact, *American Idol* is the only show in television history to be #1 in the ratings for six consecutive seasons.

Because *American Idol* is so big, it seemed a natural progression for knock-off contests to spring up across America. I was visiting a high school in another city when I saw a poster for their version of an *Idol*-like contest. It occurred to me that such a contest would not only provide a platform where my a cappella groups could perform, but would also serve as a recruitment tool for the best talent in the school.

Here's how we handled this event. Tweak as needed for your program.

» Hold open auditions for the school

- Create a poster

- Target two groups of musicians: singers and beat-boxers

- Grab a few faculty members to sit in on the cattle call

- Listen to everyone

  - Singers should sing a 60-second a cappella song (like the Golden Ticket round on *Idol)*

  - Beat-boxers should throw down a 60-second solo

- Pick your top 10 singers and top 3 beat-boxers

» Post the results from the first round of auditions

» Have the finalists come to a meeting where you will:

- Collect from them a karaoke track of predetermined length

- Hold a random drawing for performance order

- Schedule sound check times

- Reiterate rules about time limits

» Now get to work selling tickets for the actual show!

- Sell at lunch

- Sign out tickets to your group to sell

» Host the actual show

- Each ticket is a ballot (one vote per audience member)

- Winners selected by crowd vote

- Have your group perform while the vote is tallied

Now you know where some great new talent is, and lots of their friends have seen your group perform. If all goes well, your "street cred" should skyrocket! There's no question this works; I have found at least two awesome, new musicians each year through this process, and that's worth the time and effort of holding the event.

Record a CD: Why Wait?

The best thing we ever did was record a CD. Recording our first CD was like flipping the switch on our program—it has unimaginable power. At the heart of why you should record (in my humble opinion) is one sad fact . . . quality does not matter.

Well, let me clarify that statement. Quality does not matter to most people. What matters to most people is not *quality,* but the appearance of quality.

Don't get me wrong, you can't just record garbage. No one will buy garbage (or buy it for long), but if you have a credible product at all, get it in the can. Start the cycle. I like to call it "the cycle of virtual improvement."

No matter how basic a recording is, it will help your group immensely in the following ways:

1. *Self-Awareness*: No matter how many rehearsal recordings you might do, a "for sale" recording creates ridiculous self-awareness. When my kids hear themselves laying down tracks in the studio, they immediately say, "What have I been doing?" and then up their game.

2. *Public Awareness*: There is an immediate cache created as people think, "They have a CD; they must be good." Also, your group will begin to pick up gigs and recognition: "I'm calling about hiring your a cappella group. My friend played me the CD he bought when they sang for the Rotary Club last month." You can also use cuts from your CD as promotional material.

3. *Group Awareness*: In my opinion, the best part of the CD process is the eagerness of high-school kids to one-up each other. Each year, my students say, "We have to be better than last year's group. Just listen to that CD. We're going to have to work really hard." Of course, this is a bit of a wild-goose chase. Recordings allow us to capture a group at its best. With today's technology of pitch correction, digital editing, reverb, and audio effects, we can capture a group at *better than its best*. My 2008–2009 singers started their year competing with the previous group's CD, which means they were busting their tails to be better than *a studio recording*. This phenomenon brings the speed of progression up considerably.

Now we come back to my previous statement: What matters to most people is not *quality,* but the appearance of quality. By making any type of recording that is even *decent*, you create the public perception that you are at least *good*. The three types of awareness mentioned above lead directly to progress during the year. You sing around, do gigs, and sell CDs. Make sure the group knows, "If we don't sell at least

X amount of CDs, we won't be able to record our own at the end of the year." Trust me, they will find a way to make it happen.

At the end of the year, you record again—lather, rinse, repeat. All it takes is that brave first outing to get the ball rolling. So what are you waiting for?

Summary

These are just a few of the many activities you can do with your a cappella group. As you read the list again, think about whether the activities are for publicity, fundraising, or recruitment. Which serve more than one purpose? Then think about how to synergize these activities over the course of a few years. For example: you perform during the vote tally of Idol and then sell CDs after the show. You sing in the local parade and hand out fliers about your fall concert.

Activities:

- » National Anthem/Halftime Performances
- » Singing Valentines
- » Parade Floats
- » Idol
- » Recordings

CHAPTER 21

CREATING THE CULTURE

In this chapter, we will explore ways to create a culture in which your group will grow and thrive, self-correcting and improving over time. Having a small, select group provides more opportunities for student empowerment.

The Working Band Model

What high school student doesn't fantasize about becoming a rock star? Through your a cappella group, they will learn what it really means to be part of a working band. Assigning some internal jobs will not only give them a feeling of investment and ownership in the group, it will take some of the burden off you as the director. Here are some jobs that students can handle to help the cause:

Business Manager

At each rehearsal, you should reserve time for a business meeting. At that time, you'll cover a lot of details about your calendar, upcoming gigs, and musical goals. Of course, each student should keep track of such things for themselves, however; sometimes students forget, or changes come up. If you select a business manager, that student can be the first line of defense for questions that arise. They will be the student who always knows the details of your schedule, report times, what to wear, etc. If there is a change of plans between rehearsals and you need help getting the word out fast, just call your business manager.

Sound Technician

This is a fairly open-ended title. Depending on your student's level of competence (and willingness to learn), you could have this student do a range of chores from setting up and tearing down sound gear and keeping tabs on cords (that always short out), all the way to learning how to EQ the voices and overall room mix. Kids like to play with technology, that's no secret. Find a bright one and mentor them. Soon, they'll likely know more about the subject than you do!

Merchandise Manager

At some point, you might consider selling merchandise. CDs are cheaper to produce than ever as we discussed in Chapter 24 **Making A Recording**). T-shirts are also low-cost items to produce. Rather than selling cheese and sausage to raise money for your program, consider some merchandise. In my time as a director, I've seen many a gig where the merchandise sales exceeded the performance fee. A trustworthy student can keep tabs on your stock, make the right change, and be a fantastic salesperson for you. Remember all the times you bought Girl Scout cookies just to be supportive? (OK, and to eat them . . .) The same theory holds true here. Adults love to support kids, and merchandise will move.

Web Master

I'm sure there are entire books dedicated just to setting up a web presence. Considering the rapid pace at which technology evolves, we won't try to tackle all the details here. Suffice it to say that creating a website of any sort has become amazingly easy. So easy, in fact, that a student can run it for you. Whether you choose MySpace, Facebook or any number of free (or really cheap) hosting services, you can have a very functional website in no time. You can post pictures, sample audio clips, upcoming concert dates, and booking information. This becomes a great way to get kids and parents involved by submitting their own content to the picture gallery. A smart student will run rings around this job and love it. The catch? Create an account just for this purpose, so it can be passed from year to year. If you let a student set something up on their own, they might use information that is linked with their personal email and cause you some trouble in the future when it comes time to pass the torch.

Musical Leadership

I suggest to you now (and reinforce in Chapter 4 **How to Structure Your Rehearsal**) that some of the best growth your group will experience is when you are not in the room. There is no replacement for a rehearsal run by a professional (that's you), but there is a feeling of liberation that occurs when students rehearse on their own. Their guard comes down, and whatever momentum they lose due to inexperience or lack of planning is compensated for by great creative energy.

Towards that end, I suggest you have two layers of student musical leadership in large groups (more than one on a part), and one layer in small groups (one on a part).

Student Director

Self-explanatory, right? This person should be someone that has the ability to run a rehearsal in your absence, but might not be your best musician, period. The students have to respect them as a leader, too. Sometimes your #2 musician is your #1 choice for student director. Find something else valuable for #1 to do, be it business manager or section leader.

The student director doesn't create music nearly as much as they oversee goals. Whenever you rehearse together, you'll set musical goals for the following rehearsal. If there is a student-run rehearsal in-between, the student director's job is to move the ball forward on all your goals, not create their own agenda. Conversely, they should allow time in rehearsal to field and test student ideas on sounds, dynamics, choreography, etc. and narrow all those suggestions down, so that the best can be presented to you for a decision at the next rehearsal.

Another great way to lighten your load is to have each singer record a run-through to submit to the student director for note analysis. All rehearsals run smoother with everyone singing the right notes, and your SD can help maximize your time with the group by eliminating mistakes in advance.

Section Leaders

In a larger group, there could be three or four voices on a part. Why not make a qualified upperclassman a section leader? Then, each voice part can hold brief sectionals once a week to perfect notes, sharpen skills, and work on sectional blend. It also becomes a social event, bringing the singers closer together. Naming a section leader also puts some pressure on your best singers to stay on their game. Without some responsibility, students who are the best of their section might be tempted to "slack off" on their preparation for your group. It's easy for them to think, "Well, I'm already ahead of the other sopranos, so there isn't much to do until they catch up." You want your most talented singers pulling the pack forward, not sitting in the shade waiting on them to catch up.

Another benefit of having section leaders is the ability to augment your gig repertoire. If you have a group of sixteen singers, why not have the section leaders learn a few quartet numbers to keep their skills sharp? Not only will it expand your gig package, but it can be useful in those situations around school where an administrator just wants one or two songs performed, but doesn't want sixteen students pulled from class.

Student Empowerment

More than anything, students want a say. They want a voice in the direction of their group. I have found that most times, this is an undesirable and unwieldy process. Imagine if I put everything to a vote in my seventh-grade chorus of sixty kids. Chaos. Bad music. Not pretty.

However, in a small, select group of your high school's finest singers, this is a different story. There should be something that makes all the hard work they do extra-special. Having some input into the group is enticing to the current members, and is an incentive for future auditionees.

Here are a few ways of empowering students. Remember that you *always* have the final say. You won't have to lord that over your group—they understand.

Song Selection

Chapter 3 **So What Do We Sing?** includes information on allowing student input on song selection. You are a powerful team, you and your students. You have a depth of knowledge in older (classic) pop music, while they are listening to today's Top 40 non-stop. This process will allow you to learn a lot from each other and keep your set list balanced for audiences of all ages.

What to Wear

Chapter 11 **What to Wear** reminds us of the value of *themes* of clothing, rather than forced matching of outfits. Anything that matches will not look equally good on everyone. With a *theme* of clothing, each student can wear something that expresses their personality and makes their body type look good, increasing confidence and personal ownership in the group.

Planning Your Set List

Chapter 9 **Planning Your Set List** of the same name, we explore how to create a good set list. Talk your kids through the process. Explain the role of each song, and then ask each student to create their own version of a set list. Look for commonalities. It is eye-opening to see what students perceive as their strongest and weakest numbers, what they think audiences will like the most. After that, shape them through the process together and arrive on a good set list. Even if you have to exercise "veto power," you're bound to use at least a couple of their ideas.

Writing the Script

In **Planning Your Set List** we also discuss when the group should talk to the audience. After you've created the set list, come up with your planned talking points and assign each one to a student. Have them write a short script and practice it, then come ready to the next rehearsal to present if from memory.

CD Title and Artwork

Should you eventually produce a CD (and I think you should if you can), involve the students in the creative process of picking a title and/or artwork. Again, you're asking them for input, and then you make the final decision. Have them start with what they want the album to "say" to the consumer. Then work backward from that to the details. If you want the album to project "high energy," then "Hangin' Out at Lincoln High" is not a good title. A better title might be "Electrify." If that's your title, then some form of electricity is likely to appear in your artwork. You get the picture. Impressions lead to a title, which leads to artwork.

Some ideas on where to get titles:

» A title of a song on the CD

» Something that refers to your geographical location

» A phrase that seems to have stuck with the group during the year

» One word that embodies the spirit of your group

Tips about artwork:

» Once you are at the point of producing more than one CD, make sure the coloring of the artwork is different each time. That makes them easy to differentiate on the merchandise table.

» Photographs of the group will date your CD, and make it tougher to sell when your new group comes around. Photographs are best inside the CD, which can only be seen after purchase.

» Avoid putting the year of the group on the cover, for the same reason.

» Check with the CD production house to determine:

  • If they will do the artwork or if you will tackle it yourself.

  • In what format they want the artwork submitted.

Hosting Events

A great way to build teamwork, fundraise and/or serve the choir program is for your group to host an event. We expand on this in Chapter 20 **A Cappella Meets PR**, so we'll just say this: having the students assist you with the planning of (and working of) an event where they are *not* the stars is a great way to build culture. It shows the rest of your program that this is not just the "fun club for favorites" and it also gets the students to collaborate on a project that is non-musical. When they work an event, they become so much more aware of the production side of performing, something they might not consider if they are only ever on stage in the spotlight.

All in the Family: Alumni Strengthen the Program

There's no question that alumni can strengthen any program with their support. Most often, we think of alums as willing donors or as easy ticket sales for homecoming concerts. Alumni can greatly strengthen your culture if you cultivate relationships. Here's what we have found:

» *Arrangements*
  While it is a rare student who arranges music in high school, many of your best students will go off to study music in college. More free time, experience, and theory training will turn them into a great resource. Yes, there are many places to get charts, but using alumni to create legal arrangements has such a great "circle of life" quality for the singers.

» *Recording*
  One of our ex-members had always dabbled in live sound reinforcement through playing in bands. He bought some recording gear to do overdubs and demos on his guitar at home. He didn't know much about recording at the time, but it was really affordable. He cut his teeth on our first album, and very quickly became an amazing asset. He now helps with recording and runs live sound for many of our shows. Getting in on the ground

floor with someone who wants to learn the recording/live sound trade is mutually beneficial.

» *Alumni Outreach Coordinator*
We are about to get our first-ever formalized alumni organization, starting when one of our strong seniors graduates this year. She is already on board, and will live in town for the next few years—a perfect candidate to build a sustainable organization.

» *Camp Counselor*
I have many alums who come back in the summertime and sit in on our rehearsals at "a cappella camp." They help with sectionals, do one-on-one coaching, and do tech work for our end-of-week camp show.

» *Pinch-hitters*
Recently, we had a big gig in town: singing an hour slot on the 4th of July. The event usually pulls in thousands. When our bass announced he was taking a job in Germany right after graduation, I thought we'd have to cancel. The group had other ideas, and thought one step ahead to contact two alums to split the job of learning all the bass parts.

» *Assistant Directors*
If you have any alums in the area, get them to come back to rehearsals. They could come only from time to time to offer a fresh perspective as a coach or they could direct sectionals on a regular basis. One of my alums became a music major at a local university, and ended up directing my middle-school group.

This all sounds a bit obvious . . . but alums love their group. Small groups like this are high-school highlights, so they love to see the group succeed as time goes on. How wonderful for the organization to find new ways for alums to keep the group not just surviving, but *growing*. Whatever talents your alums are cultivating in college, invite them to use their old group as a risk-free training ground. Because they care about the group, they'll go above and beyond, and they'll get experience, too.

The best part about using alums is that it shows current and future members that they are part of something very special, something bigger than themselves. It also vividly illustrates that all the extra work members are putting in now will not just fade away at commencement. Members know that they are forever linked with all incarnations of their group, past and present. What's a better feeling than that?

Summary

By taking the time to consider all the possible aspects of student empowerment, from internal leadership to alumni assistance, you are creating a culture that will stay strong over the years. Not only are you allowing your students the opportunity to learn more than just notes, you are creating a network of help for when your schedule gets rough. Beyond that, you're creating a musical family. When times get tough for you or your singers, you'll be able to lean on each other and come out smiling.

CHAPTER 22

Pop A Cappella in the Classroom

with Alex Phan

Have you ever used contemporary a cappella in your classroom? If not, why? If the answer is, "because that's not the kind of choir we are," let us challenge that notion. You are a collection of vocal musicians. Musicians should not pigeon-hole themselves. Musicians should draw on every skill possible to create a great end product. Many great pop musicians have classical training, and similarly some great classical artists draw from a diverse range of other styles. Consider Bobby McFerrin, who became world-famous for the a cappella pop hit "Don't Worry, Be Happy," but also directed the St. Paul Chamber Orchestra. Similarly, Paul McCartney wrote the *Liverpool Oratorio*. Music is music. In order to help students grow, we have to break the mentality that musicians are divided into "camps" and do not, will not, cross over. We also have to smash the stereotype that says that different genres of music have different values. Greatness and mediocrity exist in all types of music.

I'm not here to say that you HAVE to use pop music in your classroom—just be open to the idea. I'm not even saying you have to perform pop music on your concert. After all, you don't have to perform every bit of music you learn, do you?

Why Do We Program the Music We Program?

When you pick music for your curricular choirs, why do you pick it? I'm assuming that you pick songs that are educationally appropriate. You consider the key signature, time signature, amount of accidentals, range of the singers, and so on. You probably also consider what will be interesting to the audience. Certainly you consider what will be exciting for the students and engaging for you as the director. Finally, you consider what fits the "vibe" of the choir. Your madrigal group wouldn't sing *Carmina Burana*, for instance.

Having said all that, let's think about pop music. Pop music is *diverse*. Are there songs or arrangements that can carry your educational tenets forward? *Yes*. Interesting to the audience? *Yes*. Exciting and engaging? *Yes*. Fits the "vibe" of your choir? Let's explore that further.

Eating a Balanced Diet

We're about to take a tour through an extended analogy, so hang in there . . .

Old-Fashioned Cooking

Generations of kids grew up hearing a familiar refrain: "If you don't eat your dinner, you can't have dessert." In the choir world, we often see directors positioning genres of music this way. "Our curricular choirs sing more classical music (dinner) and our after-school groups get to sing pop (dessert)." Perhaps we do ourselves a disservice by keeping this mantra alive. After all, great music is great music.

Old-fashioned cooking is simple. It's intense within the simplicity. Imagine a dinner of roast beef with mashed potatoes, carrots, and gravy. What words come to mind? Heavy. Thick. Starchy. Hearty. Now imagine what dessert might follow such a dinner—apple pie à la mode. Sweet. Syrupy. Decadent. Neither one of these courses is balanced. It isn't to say that they can't be good, can't be tasty. They are good and they compliment each other.

Consider the musical paradigm that exists in so many schools: chamber choir is "dinner" and pop music (or gospel, show choir, barbershop, a cappella, etc.) is "dessert." It would certainly get old to eat nothing but roast beef, and it would get equally boring to eat nothing but apple pie. Consider now that any student who is only in one performing ensemble is eating a very unbalanced diet. How can we improve this scenario? Well, I wouldn't suggest you try to create "roast beef a la mode," that's for sure. I would suggest moving first into the "hidden-ingredient" paradigm and then eventually into "gourmet cooking," both of which will be explained next.

Hidden Ingredients

You might remember a while back there was a small hub-bub about two cookbooks, *Deceptively Delicious* and *The Sneaky Chef*. The claim was that one plagiarized the other. Both explained that a great way to improve the diets of kids was to "hide" good foods inside traditional kid favorites. Examples included cauliflower puree inside mac and cheese and spinach inside brownies.

A great way to energize your choirs is to adopt this strategy with their music. Students love pop music. That's just life. How can you use that to your advantage? Sprinkle it into aspects of your rehearsal as a way to soften the usual resistance to training exercises like warm-ups and sight-reading. Here are a few examples:

1. *Vocal Percussion to Help Rhythm Reading*

    During warm-ups, we often do diction exercises like "the lips, the teeth, the tip-of-the-tongue" or "red leather, yellow leather." Try some simple kick drum, snare drum, and high-hat rhythms. Your students will love it, but make it simple! Repeat patterns of four-quarter notes on different vocal percussion instruments. Four kicks: "buh, buh, buh, buh." Four snares: "kih, kih, kih, kih." Four high hats: "tik, tik, tik, tik."

Now read a simple rhythm and you're off to the races. Assign instrument syllables to specific notes for your rhythmic training. Quarter notes are kicks, eighth notes are snares, and rests are high hats. Run through your rhythms with vocal percussion. The kids are having a great time and still learning the fundamentals of music. Advanced version: create rhythm patterns that one section can do while other sections sing scales or vocalises. Trade so everyone gets a turn.

2. *Sight-reading = Spontaneous Combustion*

I once listened to the local hip-hop station during my commute and heard the song "Firework," recorded by Katy Perry. The solo line, "'Cause baby, you're a firework," was simply "low sol, high sol, fa, mi, re, re, do mi." I turned it into the daily sight-reading. Everyone was pretty lethargic when reading the example at first. I had the class read it slowly and then began to speed it up in repetition. Eventually I added a bass line and sang some backup harmonies. Pretty soon eyes began to light up. Eventually someone raised their hand and said, "Is this 'Firework?'" The energy in the room shifted and the rest of the rehearsal was exciting and successful. Sure, the whole ordeal was fabricated in order to get the kids to love what they were doing. We're all guilty of that. Why do we show our kids choir videos? Why do we play clips of the Robert Shaw Chorale singing masterworks? *To get them excited!* With pop a cappella in our arsenal, we have extra ammo for our choral battle.

3. *Getting the New Kids Hooked on Singing in Warm-ups*

Yet another example points to the necessity of enticement during the first week of school. I use this technique from year to year without hesitation. Kodaly began using well-known folk songs to teach musical literacy. Today's popular tunes are our equivalent to Kodaly's songs. My two personal "go-to" songs are "Many the Miles" by Sara Bareilles and "Billy Jean" by Michael Jackson. For each, teach the bass line and then the backup harmonies. Create both parts yourself for authenticity. Sing them over and over as your warm-up. Then play the original. Again, with a simple bass line and two easy harmonies, you've created the idea that each kid can produce the same product that is heard on the radio. You'll begin to hear, "Can we do this on our concert?" or "We should learn the whole song!" While you might not sing those songs on a concert, you can create warm-ups that rock or even just something fun to sing whenever energy is getting low in rehearsal. It's easy to forget that singing is fun, and there's nothing wrong with singing something fun just to restore morale.

4. *Theory Work with a Goal*

Why not make a deal with the choir that you'll sing a song if they can arrange it? Maybe it's for the spring concert. Break the choir into groups, and then break the song project into parts that they can achieve while you maintain a regular rehearsal schedule. If there are four groups in the choir, there are four songs they can perform on the final show. The kids love the songs and you can tell the audience that everything they hear was written by the students on stage. Sounds like a win-win!

Week 1: Notate the melody of the song.

Week 2: Notate the bass line.

Week 3: Determine and mark the chord structure (like a lead sheet).

Week 4: Craft and notate backing vocals within the chord structure.

Gourmet Cooking

There are many popular cooking shows on TV today. Some of them include *Top Chef, Chopped, Kitchen Nightmares,* and *Hell's Kitchen.* It is not uncommon to see some unusual recipes on these shows (or in high-end restaurants if you go there). Gourmet cooking strives for balance. Rarely will you see just meat and potatoes. That's considered too heavy. Many spices or even sweet ingredients are used to lighten the feel of the entree. One example would be pork chops with an apple-cider glaze. On the flip-side, desserts are often constructed to have more depth than just "sweet." A well-crafted key lime pie has tart and sweet together. I've even seen avocado-bacon ice cream.

Much like gourmet cooking, we can meld ingredients together to enhance our music. Going just one step outside your box can add variety to a concert. The King's Singers have a madrigal-ized version of "Can't Buy Me Love" by the Beatles. That's a charming way to catch the audience off guard when your chamber choir performs. There's an 8-part choral setting of "Somewhere" from West Side Story as well. In that vein, why not find a popular ballad and create a choral setting of it? The results could be very moving. What if you did an opera-chorus version of Justin Bieber's "Baby?" I think it could bring the house down with laughter. What about an a cappella setting of a popular song like "You Raise Me Up" or "Home" for commencement? The King's Singers' arrangement of "MLK" by U2 is wonderful for chamber choirs or pop groups alike. More and more we find that the right popular music (in the right setting) can be immensely effective in a traditional concert choir format.

The opposite side of that coin is to have your a cappella group do some classical singing, or at least a "gourmet cooking" version of it. A Swingle Singers' arrangement of a classical piece will allow your a cappella group to drop a dash of culture into their program, and can even be a novelty number with some light-hearted choreography. You could also perform world music, which is often rhythmic and complex. Another fun idea is to take a popular song and arrange it in many styles. I once heard a barbershop quartet sing "My Darling Clementine" as if it were done by the Beach Boys, then Motown, then opera, then barbershop. It brought the house down. Could you do the same with a song your group chooses?

Summary

» Athletes cross-train. Shouldn't musicians?

» Take time to consider your programming habits (or ruts) and break out of them.

» Use popular music to create variety and reach kids in a way you hadn't thought possible.

» Don't view musical styles in black and white. Explore the gray areas and think outside the box.

» When students want to sing popular songs, use that to your advantage as an educational challenge.

CHAPTER 23

The Feeder Program

In this chapter, we will discuss the benefits of a feeder program. We all understand why the basketball team has both a varsity and a junior-varsity squad. We take great care to nurture our middle school choirs to become the high school singers of tomorrow. Why not apply the same concept to your a cappella group? Once you have an a cappella group for any length of time, student demand will likely far outstrip the available slots each year at auditions. Rather than turn talented (but less experienced) singers aside, start a feeder group.

Benefits of a Feeder Group

Excitement

There's nothing more exciting than achievement and progress. One way athletic teams keep kids working hard is by giving them the opportunity to advance in level as they progress. Players advance up the ladder from *freshman* to *junior varsity* to *varsity*. By installing a feeder group, you offer students the opportunity to climb the musical ladder. A talented freshman could make your JV group and then be motivated all year long towards moving up. If you have a group of 12, what happens to students 13–28 after they fail to make the cut? They *might* regroup and work towards a better audition next year, but a feeder group guarantees they are growing. They have supervision, motivation, and purpose. They are practicing to improve their group, which means they are simultaneously improving themselves.

The Extended Audition

A feeder group offers the "next wave" of talent an extended audition. By working with them for a year before they hit the big leagues, you'll discover all the non-musical attributes that make a student an asset to any group:

» Commitment to practice outside rehearsal

» Punctuality

» Team spirit

» Leadership

» Responsibility

» Representation of the program to the public

The singers in the feeder group also get a chance to learn more about how your a cappella program works. Some students think they want to do it, but when they get in and see it isn't just a karaoke club, they change their minds. And if a cappella is something they love, they'll be inspired to work harder than ever to move forward.

Microphone Technique and Technical Skills

Singing on a sound system is something that requires practice. A feeder group not only allows your students to develop singing skills, but also affords them the opportunity to hone microphone technique. Another benefit is that one of the feeder group kids might show an aptitude for running the sound board, and could assist with your top group by becoming a sound engineer.

Gigs

Performances are worth ten practices, easy. Students love to perform, and are highly motivated to do better when they know they'll be in front of an audience. Gigs for your feeder program give the "next wave" of singers more motivation to grow.

Parent Involvement

Great programs have great parent support. Feeder groups help cultivate parent booster relationships early on. Feeder groups need chaperones, fundraisers, and all other kinds of help. Get your kids in the pipeline early and their parents will come along for the ride.

Food for the Tigers

I've always been told, "You have to feed the tigers." The best students are always looking for a challenge. They would rather push themselves than get bored. A feeder group allows advanced younger students a place to work at a faster pace and achieve their fullest potential.

Types of Feeders

The Junior-Varsity Group

One version of a feeder group is having an identical version of your top group, only younger. If you have a top group that is a mixed octet, another mixed octet could work well, allowing members to get used to that style of singing. Another option is to have the same voicing, but a larger group of students. Our program has a mixed octet as the top group, and a mixed group of 16 as the feeder.

If you have the time and want to get a lot of students in the pipeline, you could have two JV groups—one for men and one for women. This presumes your top group is mixed. The benefits include a lot of student involvement and having three distinct types of repertoire represented at your concerts.

The Middle School Group

A middle school group might sound daunting, but is very achievable. The biggest challenge comes from vocal ranges (harder to find low basses especially). If you have the ability to arrange for them (or re-voice existing arrangements), you can make this work quite well. I have had success with a small group of eight on hand-held microphones, and also with a large group of 16 on zone mics. The larger group was actually voiced SSAT, with the tenors singing a "bass line" in the lower part of their range. While some of the rhythms in a cappella can be complex, if the arrangement is constructed with the same background parts repeated regularly, younger students should be able to easily learn it.

Curricular Inserts

If you don't have the time or energy to have another group, you could instead sprinkle some pop a cappella pieces into your concert repertoire. They make great closers at almost any program, but could also be a larger piece of a spring program. Students enjoy them and you can use some of the techniques listed in Chapter 22 **Pop A Cappella in the Classroom** to make them educational experiences.

Strategies to Strengthen Your Feeder

Combined Numbers

Plan a few easier songs that your top group and feeder group can sing together. You can sing them as a "mega-group" for big school events (like football games) or short community engagements where no amplification is available. Also, if your top group has a short gig opportunity and one of your singers has a conflict, you can "call someone up from the minors" to fill in. That's a win on so many levels.

Joint Performances

Sometimes you'll get a call to provide entertainment and the client wants more music than you have prepared. I have had many clients who want a full hour of music in October or November. In these situations, taking both groups along to fill that time will satisfy the client and provide a great bonding experience for your students. The feeder group can also "learn the ropes" while they are mentored by your top group.

Training Gigs

Sometimes you just have to invent reasons to get your kids in front of an audience. There are many ways to drum up gigs mentioned in Chapter 15 **Moving to the Stage**. Finding low-stress gigs for your feeder group affords them an opportunity to learn the art of performance with minimal risk.

Recording Bonus Tracks

Let's say your top group is recording a CD. Have your feeder group record one or two of its best songs for inclusion as bonus tracks. Those singers are now learning how to record before they hit the top group, and the CD will have a larger sales base as you include the family and friends of the feeder group. When the feeder group sings a gig, they also have something to sell, and that helps your program's bottom line.

Social Time

Get your groups to hang out together. Over time, your top group members will be able to offer some insight as to what the various feeder group singers are like. I'm not advising you to just take a student's word at face value. I will say, however, that sometimes student insight can help you when it comes time to make tough audition decisions.

Summary

In building a solid culture that will last for years to come, a feeder group is an essential tool. Students and parents all have a way to get involved sooner and grow together more over time. If you don't have the bandwidth to run the feeder group yourself, consider hiring an alum or college music major to help.

CHAPTER 24

Making A Recording
by Freddie Feldman

So you want to make an a cappella album? A cappella groups have been recording and releasing albums for decades, but not until recently has it been so relatively easy and inexpensive to accomplish. And just because it is easier and cheaper doesn't mean groups are doing it any more successfully than before.

Like any problem, there are many ways to get to the solution. Mine is just one way. I've produced over 80 a cappella CDs in the past twelve years and I see groups making the same mistakes over and over again. These mistakes can be costly, annoying, and even tragic.

I'm not going to talk much about production techniques—all of the stuff that happens in the studio. In my opinion, you don't need to know very much about that. You're going to be paying recording engineers, mixers, producers, and mastering engineers to handle those details. You need to know how to put it all together, on time and on budget. I'll show you how to predictably get a finished album in your hands by your due date.

I'm not just pulling these methods out of the air or basing them solely on observations. I have actually used them myself. In December 2005, I released the *Dark Side of the Moon A Cappella*. I acted as not only the producer on this album, but also the vocal percussionist, one of the soloists, and the record label. It was my responsibility to make sure this project was managed properly. And why not? Tens of thousands of my own dollars were at stake and I couldn't afford to lose it all. After years of teaching groups how to manage their own recording projects, it was my turn to make good on my promises of success!

Even though it was a massive album to coordinate, the *Dark Side* CD went off pretty much without a hitch. The one or two bumps that I encountered in the road were aptly dodged because I had planned ahead and I was prepared for the worst.

Keep two things in mind as you read this chapter and begin the process of making your own album: plan ahead and have fun. Follow those two rules and everything else will fall into place.

Thinking Ahead

The number one rule of making an album is: *plan ahead.*

That's it, we're done. Good luck with your CD! Just kidding, but only a little. There's a lot to know but if you always plan ahead, you'll be prepared. If you don't plan ahead, what are you going to do when Mr. Murphy (see Murphy's Law) pays you a visit with a phone call telling you that your artwork "is going to delay production because of a problem with the ink density?" You're going to be out of luck. Plain and simple.

Before you do anything, sit down and plan out the project. It doesn't have to take hours and hours, but "wingin' it" isn't a good plan when you have thousands of dollars (and your reputation) at stake.

If you know all the steps of the process, you'll know how to plan accordingly. Let's look at a typical list of milestones in the average recording project. We'll go into how to schedule these milestones in the next sections. First, let's see what tasks we are scheduling:

» Planning

» Tracking

» Editing/Mixing

» Mastering

» Artwork Preparation

» Licensing Preparation

» Pressing/Printing

» Distribution/Promotion

Why Record an Album in the First Place?

Yearbook

Scholastic groups tend to record one album a year and it represents a year in the life of the group.

Product

Turn an unpaid gig into a paying one (groups will usually sell 70% of their CDs at shows). Sure, sometimes you have to play a show for free (or close to it). But if you've got a decent-looking product to sell at the show, you can still make some money for your program.

Choosing an Album Title

The sooner you can start talking about what you are going to call your album, even what order your songs will be in, the better. You will have many differing opinions within your group. Choosing an album title will take longer than you think. START EARLY!

Many times the album name is some inside joke within the group. Sometimes an album name will embody the feeling the group had while making the album. Get creative! It can be one word, one sentence, one song title . . . anything!

If you get stuck, and you haven't already done this on an earlier album, you could always eponymously name your album (i.e. give the album title the same name as your group).

Choosing a Song Order

Choosing a song order does not have to be an arduous process. One helpful tip: Put the name of each song on a Post-It® note, with other info about the song (gender of soloist, tempo, key). Then put them on the wall and move them around to try out different song orders.

Everyone has their own theory about how to order the songs on your album. My personal opinion: this is not a set-list for a show. This is an album. You don't need to pace the album in the same way you'd pace a show. Don't put your super-amazing-standing-ovation song last! At a show, 99% of the people will stay to the end and get to hear that great song. On an album, they may never get that far!

Put a really strong (not strongest) song first, before mellowing it back a bit. Then hit them with your big hit as track #3 or #4. Look at your favorite commercial albums and you'll see the same thing. Put an interesting track last. Bury your weakest song just before that one.

If things start to get heated and people seriously can't agree on an order, remember that, nowadays, listeners can purchase one song at a time or play their entire collection on shuffle. Song order isn't nearly as important as it used to be.

Scheduling

The best way to make sure you get everything done on time is to work out a schedule for the whole project. There's no better way to find out where you're going than to start out looking at your destination. Work backwards. Start from your release date and work in reverse, in one-week blocks. Here's a very loose example:

Timeframe	Task
Week 17	CD Release Show
Week 16	Safety Padding
Week 12–15	Manufacturing
Week 11	Proofing & Licensing
Week 10	Artwork Preparation
Week 9	Mastering
Week 5-8	Mixing
Week 1-4	Tracking

However, isolating each task is not the fastest, most efficient use of your time. Several of the tasks can be done simultaneously. Let's consider the tasks as being in two separate parallel timelines. One set of tasks will be called "Audio" and one will be "Manufacturing." Let's take a look at the newer, more efficient timeline:

Timeframe	Audio Task	Manufacturing Task
Week 14	CD Release Show	
Week 13	Safety Padding	
Week 9–12	Manufacturing	
Week 8 (1 day)	Mastering	
Week 5–8	Mixing	Proofing & Licensing
Week 1–4	Tracking	Artwork Preparation

These are just rough estimates. It could take our group eight weeks to get everything together, rather than four. Only use this as a general guideline.

Track/Song Matrix

Never rely on your memory, or that of your studio engineer to remember which people/sections have recorded their parts in the studio. Use a chart and check off parts as you go. Then you can see your current status at a glance:

	Song #1	Song #2	Song #3	Song #4	Song #5
Solo	X	X		X	X
Harmony					
VP	X	X	X		NA
Soprano I	X	X			X
Soprano II		X		X	X
Alto I	X	X		X	X
Alto II	X	X			X
Tenor I		X	X		
Tenor II			X		
Bass I	X	X			X
Bass II	X	X	X	NA	X

Here's what the Track Matrix looked like for the *Dark Side of the Moon A Cappella* CD project:

		Track #1 Breathe	Track #2 OnTheRun	Track #3 Time	Track #4 Great Gig	Track #5 Money	Track #6 Us Them	Track #7 Any Colour	Track #8 Brain Damage
Tracking	MIDI	X	X	X	X	X	X	X	X
	Solo	Mike	N/A	Time	Steph 10/8	Freddie	X	N/A	Alan
	Soprano 1	X / X	X	X / X	X	X	X	10/8	X
	Soprano 2	/ X	X	X / X	X	X	X	10/9	10/9
	Alto 1	X / X	X	X / X	X	X	X	X	X
	Tenor 1	X / X	X	X / X	X	X	X	X	X
	Tenor 2	X /X	X	X / X	X	X	N/A	X	X
	Baritone	X / X	X	X / X	X	X	X	X	N/A
	Bass	X / X	X	X / X	X	X	X	X	X
	VP	/ X				X			
	Extra								
Mixing	Draft 1	Thursday / X	Thursday	/ X	X	Saturday	X	Friday	X
	Draft 2	X	X	X	X	X	X	X	X
	Draft 3	X	X	X	X	X	X	X	X
	Draft 4	X	X	X	N/A	X	N/A	N/A	X
	Final	X	X	X	X	X	X	X	X

Budgeting

You must setup a realistic budget for your recording project, and do it *before* you actually get into the studio. Find out all costs up front, so that there are no surprises later. Always add some breathing room to your budget (sometimes called "padding") for the unexpected hours/costs that will invariably come up.

I've put this section first because you should do your budget first. If some of the terms are unfamiliar to you, try skipping this section and coming back to it later.

Tracking

Discuss this one with your recording studio and producer/mixer. Ask them for an average of how many hours will it take to record one song. Then multiply it all out:

# of songs × *hours per song* × *hourly rate* = **recording budget**

Editing

If your mixer uses a separate editor, you will have to budget their time as well. This calculation is done like you calculated for tracking.

Mixing

This one is pretty much the same as tracking. Find out how many hours, on average, it will take to mix one song. Then multiply.

Mastering

If you choose to have your producer/mixer master your album, let them know ahead of time and find out how much it will cost. It should run you about $300-$500 for a basic album. A full-time mastering studio will charge you anywhere from $300 to $2000 to master your album. It's usually 30–45 minutes per song at a rate of $75–$475 per hour. So, count on maybe 5–6 hours for a 12-song album. Find out *all* mastering costs up front. Some studios will charge you a separate fee to burn the finished master. Most studios will charge you a media fee for the blank CD-Rs, and some will charge you an archiving fee as well.

Artwork/Photography

Figure this into your budget as well. Who will be preparing the artwork for your CD? Will you need any photos taken of the group? Many times you can get someone you know to do this for you for free.

Legal/Licensing

I discuss the details of this later, but if you have covered any tunes on your album, you will be required to pay Mechanical Licenses in order to put them on your CD. You must pay this fee up front when you manufacture your CDs, and you pay based on the number of CDs printed, not the number of CDs you sell. The rate is 9.1-cents per song, per copy printed. You will also pay a $10 service fee for each song you license. So if you have 12 covered tunes on your album, plan on paying about $1200 for 1000 copies.

Replication

I would set aside a full $2000 for replicating 1000 CDs. You can find cheap places that will do it for $1000, but you'd better be really on the ball and know what you're doing. I usually recommend Discmakers, since I am a Platinum Studio Partner with them (mention VOCOMOTION when you place your order).

Keep in mind that you will pay taxes and shipping on your CD order. Shipping 1000 CDs can be more expensive than you would think. Ask your manufacturer up front about the average shipping costs (and sales tax rate) for the number of CDs you will be ordering.

Recording/Mixing

I'm not going to talk too much about the recording and mixing process itself. You will be paying someone to handle those details. I'll give you some information on selecting a producer/mixer, and a studio, and then delve into some administrative issues that often arise during the recording/mixing process.

The two things that will occur during the part of the process are: tracking and mixing. Tracking is the process of actually recording your tracks. Mixing is adjusting levels of various sounds on a song. This also may include editing and adding effects/processing.

Producer vs. Mixer?

I keep writing "producer/mixer" because you may use either a producer or a mixer to mix your CD. A mixer is a person who will simply mix your album, based on their expertise at mixing a cappella. A producer can also mix your album but they may also, at times, help you with other aspects of your album production, including song production, songwriting, arranging, and other tasks.

Finding a Producer/Mixer

I urge you to find a qualified and experienced producer/mixer who has worked on a cappella recordings before. This person does not necessarily need to live anywhere near you (or even in the same hemisphere). First, I'll recommend you use me as your producer (hey, it's my chapter!). I do have several friends in the industry who also produce a cappella albums exclusively that I could recommend, should you wish to explore other options.

Remote Production

There are only so many people out there with the right skills and experience to properly produce your album. If you do not live near one of these rare people, don't despair! It has become very popular to record your tracks where you are and send them out to have someone produce/mix them remotely. You may either use a local studio, or you could even do the recording on your own.

If you have the resources, I would still recommend going to a local studio for tracking your parts. They will almost always have better gear and they will have experience recording vocals. If you do not intend to mix your tracks in the same studio that you record the tracks, you must let the tracking studio know up front of your intentions.

Things to Discuss with Your Producer/Mixer

What are your goals for this album?

Why are you recording this album? Are you planning on selling it? How detailed/ picky do you want to be with tuning, rhythm, and mixing?

How many songs will you be recording?

This seems unimportant, but it can be often overlooked. Be sure your producer/ mixer has time in their schedule to mix all the tracks you wish to have on the album.

What kind of sound are you going for?

Bring some recorded tracks of other a cappella groups you like. Heck, bring some non-a cappella tracks too. The more specific you can be about what you like, the better. Do you like a heavily-produced sound? Lots of effects? No effects? A more live sound? No pitch correction (Autotune/Melodyne)? No vocal percussion? Organic vocal percussion? Synthetic vocal percussion? These are all important things to discuss before you start recording a single take.

Will there be anyone else mixing any of the tracks?

Some groups like to sample different producers on the same album. They may have one producer work on three songs, another on three songs, etc. Personally, I think the album doesn't flow very well when it is produced by so many various people. I feel an album should be thought of as a complete product and should have a consistent sound/feel as a whole. I have, however, been a part of albums where I only mixed three or four tracks. It just depends on the group and the album.

Do you plan to use any other pre-recorded material?

Some groups can't afford to record a full 12-song album, and want to include some pre-recorded live recordings (maybe from last year's Spring Show) to beef-up the CD. Let your producer/mixer know that ahead of time. Some producers may not be into having these tracks on the album; some may really dig it.

Mastering

Mastering is the final step in the process of making a recording, before it goes to manufacturing. Contrary to a common misconception, **no mixing is done during mastering**. The audio for your album is processed as a final mix to "finish" or "sweeten" the audio. Do not ever count on mastering to fix any mixing, tuning, or other such issues in the recording. "They'll fix it in mastering" is not a valid excuse for bad mixes.

Your recording studio will provide "pre-masters," which are finished mixes of your recordings, ready to be mastered. The mastering studio will then look at your album as a whole. It's good to have another set of ears listens to the mixes and maybe identify some over-arching issues with the mixes. They may be a little muddy in the bottom-end, and they can try to fix this. Maybe they're not bright enough overall.

This can be adjusted as well. Things they can't usually fix: the solo is too loud or soft, the rhythm of the vocal percussionist is off, sopranos are flat, and other such mixing issues.

The mastering studio will also boost the volume of your tracks, to get them as hot (loud) as possible. In order to crank the volume as much as possible, they will have to limit the dynamics of your recording. For pop/rock songs, this will most likely be fine. If you've got more traditional choral or acoustic a cappella tracks, you may wish to keep as much of your dynamic contrast as possible. Just let your mastering engineer know what you expect, and they should be able to accommodate you.

Why Can't They Just Make it Sound Perfect in the Mixing?

Well, nobody's perfect. Your producer will get your mix to sound great, but the mastering studio will make your album sound like an album. They have special gear that is very different from the gear used in mixing. If the mixes are good, the mastering studio won't have to do very much.

Making the Master CD

The final step in the mastering process is the creation of the final master CD. You will need to provide your mastering engineer with a final track order for your album. The studio will then sequence your tracks in this order, and produce a final CD-R with your master. This is not exactly like a CD you might burn in iTunes. It will be a PMCD. The mastering studio will put special codes into this disc that the manufacturer will use to ensure the CD is replicated properly. Nowadays, manufacturers will take regular CD-Rs as masters. I've even heard of people submitting CD-Rs that were mastered burned in iTunes. This will generally turn out fine, but be warned that if you have special requirements, like tracks that flow from one to the other (no break between songs), you really want a PMCD master.

The mastering studio will also check your PMCD to make sure there are no errors on the disc. Even though CDs are digital, burning audio to them does not mean that errors will not occur. Checking your PMCD for errors will ensure your replicated discs are as close to perfect as possible.

Who Should Do the Mastering?

I highly recommend finding a separate mastering studio from the recording studio that mixed your album. Even if your recording engineer says they can master the CD for you, kindly decline this service. Tell the recording engineer that you completely trust their mastering abilities, but you'd like to have a fresh set of ears do the mastering. Your recording will thank you for it in the end (okay, it won't literally thank you, but you know what I mean).

How Do I Find a Mastering Studio?

First, ask your producer or mix engineer if they could recommend a mastering studio. Many producers work regularly with the same mastering engineer, because they work well together. I personally have a very good relationship with a mastering studio that I use for almost every project I produce. We save a lot of time because we both know the other one's expectations and work methods.

What Should it Cost?

Mastering studios charge a wide range of rates for their services. They may charge as little as $60/hour and as much as $475/hour for mastering an album. Keep in mind that these rates seem very high, but you are only paying for a few hours of work. A typical 12-song a cappella album, if mixed well and consistently, should only take three to five hours to master.

CD Manufacturing

Once your album is mixed and mastered, you need to have CDs manufactured (unless, of course, you're doing an online-only release). The manufacturing process can be tricky and takes just as long as the making of music on your album. You should start planning for manufacturing early. You can even start on the same day you start recording and work in parallel.

Replication vs. Duplication

Duplication (CD-R)

Recordable CDs (also known as CDR or CD-R) are manufactured blank. Your artwork is either printed on the surface of the disc with an inkjet or silkscreened, as with pressed CDs. The data is written ("burned" is also an acceptable term) onto them at your leisure, usually with desktop burners or stand-alone duplicators.

Recordable CDs are ideally suited for projects where you need a small quantity of one title. For example, you may want to publish one-of-a-kind recordings for fans on CDs that have the look of a mass-produced title. It is also for when your data changes frequently. Recordable media is more expensive than pressing CDs, so use it only when the project calls for it.

Caveat for CD-R Duplication: Many older car-stereos and home CD-players are not able to play burned CD-Rs. By going with replication, instead of CD-R duplication, you will ensure that the most number of people will be able to play your album successfully.

Replication (Pressed CD)

Pressed CD manufacturing differs from recordable CD burning in one very important respect. In CD pressing, all the data is put into the disc in one "stamping" or "pressing" step (called plating) using a glass master created from your CD-R master. The disc shape is then created by injection molding. Once they are molded, pressed CDs are either silkscreened or offset printed, and then finally inserted into their packaging.

Finding a Manufacturer

Discmakers (www.discmakers.com) and Oasis CD (www.oasiscd.com) are two of the largest CD manufacturers for independent releases. I know there might be cheaper alternatives (not that much cheaper), but if you can possibly afford it, go with one of the larger manufacturers. They are much more organized and will be less likely to completely screw up your project (although it could happen with any of them). Let your account representative know your deadlines at the beginning! You may even want to lie a little about the deadline (by a week). Padding your schedule is always a good thing.

How Many CDs Should We Order?

Order what you think you could possibly sell within a couple years, not how many you'll sell before your next CD comes out. You won't sell them all in a year, but you will still have people buying them several years later.

The smallest quantity most manufacturers will accept is 300 or 500. Don't order these smaller quantities if you can afford to possibly get 1,000. The price difference, per CD, between quantities under 1,000 and over 1,000 are significant. Many companies will actually print 1,000 copies even if you order 500. It costs about the same for them. Then, later, when you need 500 more CDs, they will sell them to you at a "discounted re-order price." They set the price-break at 1000 for a reason; use it.

When Should We Place a Re-order for More CDs?

Plan ahead and you'll never be without discs. Don't wait until you have ten CDs left to order more. Set an amount, and when you hit that amount, order more. You really need to base this on how fast you're selling your album right now. Take your average album sales per week, multiply that by five, and that's how many CDs you should have left when you place your re-order.

Let's say you ordered 1,000 CDs to start. You're selling 20 CDs a week. That means that you should re-order more discs when you have 100 CDs remaining. This way, if you continue to sell 20 discs each week, you'll be covered for the three weeks it might take to get your next re-ordered batch of CDs. I've padded it a little, because you never know when you're going to sell a bunch more.

Freddie's Rule: You never want to be completely out of discs. If you don't have any CDs, you're not going to sell any CDs. If you plan ahead, and are able to refresh your supply just before you run out, you'll be all set!

Packaging Options

Nowadays, all of the major manufacturers offer a variety of interesting packaging options. The two main choices are Jewelcases and DigiPaks. The Jewelcase is a standard plastic CD case. DigiPaks are those cardboard cases (not cardboard sleeves though, as in CD singles).

Recommendation for scholastic groups: Go with the 4-panel folder. It's the cheapest and it will have enough room to fit all of your information. You're probably not doing many original songs, so you won't be including lyrics (remember, you're not allowed to print the lyrics of cover tunes without negotiating permission ahead of time).

Would it Be Better to Do an EP?

EP stands for Extended Play and, ironically, they are shorter than a regular album (LP). A standard album has 12 tracks. An EP is usually five to nine tracks. Here's why an EP may not be the greatest idea for you: it costs the same amount to press an EP as it does an LP. Of course, it will cost more to record/mix/master the extra tracks, but once you've pressed your CD, those costs are not ongoing.

Usually, you want to price your album at about a dollar per song. That would mean that you would probably only charge about $7–$9 for your EP, but still carry the same cost of manufacturing. I'm not saying to add songs just so you can charge more for your CD. Actually, I believe that scholastic a cappella albums longer than 13 or 14 tracks are just too long. But, I do believe that recording only eight songs because you'd save the money on recording is not correct.

What Must You Provide to the Manufacturer?

Artwork Files

Get their templates in the format of the software you will be using to create the artwork. FOLLOW THE MANUFACTURER'S SPECS! They will tell you the resolution (usually 300dpi) and color-space (usually CMYK). Follow the guidelines on the template exactly—they're not kidding with that stuff. I've seen some wacky results from groups that didn't provide artwork at the correct resolution.

Ink Density is something that can cause a snag in your plans. The paper that your booklet/DigiPak/etc. is printed on will actually absorb some of the ink printed on it, and will darken once it dries. Ink density is calculated by adding up the individual percentages of your darkest CMYK color. So if your darkest color has a CMYK value of 50% 60% 20% 80%, you'd add those up and get 210. Most manufacturers want you to stay under 300 or 280, so you'd be fine in this case. If you want "black," don't do 100% black, because that would add up to an Ink Density of 400. You'd have to do something like 70% 70% 70% 70%, which would add up to 280. Don't worry; your black will still be black even though it might seem like grey on the computer screen. The ink will absorb into the paper, become darker, and will look black in the end.

Use Photoshop for images. Use Freehand or Illustrator for layout and text. Photoshop is not the best program for text. Also, don't use weird programs that the manufacturer doesn't support.

On the album-cover, make the album-title smaller than the group name. The largest text will be what people think is the group name. If you make the album-title larger, people will be confused. I've seen it happen many times.

If you are a scholastic group, *please* put your school's name on the back cover somewhere (it can be small). There's nothing worse than having a listener try and figure out which "Accidentals" or "Chordials" or "Acafellas" you are.

Make sure your artwork has the approval of any governing body that supports your group. Find out if you need any approval, AS SOON AS POSSIBLE.

Master CD

Your mastering studio must provide the proper media for the master. Exabyte tape (not used much anymore), CD-R, or DAT.

Payment

Sounds so obvious, but this is no joke. The manufacturer won't even open the package you sent them (artwork, etc.) without at least your deposit. They will not go to press without having your full payment in their hands. They will also not go to press without the proofed/approved artwork and the master CD. Everything is done as one job: CDs, booklets, stuffing cases, shrink-wrapping, etc. Remember to figure shipping into your cost (1000 CDs can weigh a lot).

If you go with a foreign manufacturer (using Canadian manufacturers is getting more popular here in the States), figure in extra time for getting the CDs through customs (this can take up to a week). You may also be required to add the text "Printed in Canada" to the outside of the booklet (so customs can see it).

Unders/Overs

Your CD manufacturer will print 5% more discs than you order, in case some of the cases or discs get mangled by the machines during pressing. In the end, the quantity of finished CDs you will receive will be within 5% of the ordered amount (from 950 to 1050, if you ordered 1000). You are credited back the money for the CDs that weren't printed, and usually will be given the extra CDs for free, if you pay in full before manufacturing begins.

You may also receive many extra booklets or traycards. Be creative with these. Use them on your merchandise table to promote your new album. Be prepared to receive NO extra printed materials as well.

Album Credits/Liner Notes

Liner notes are the printed text inside of the CD packaging. This also includes any printing on the disc and in the tray card. This can be a bit of a thorny issue for some groups. Start working on it early, so that you're not waiting at the end to get all the "Thank You" lists from everyone.

Song Information

You should definitely list all of the songs on your CD, in the order they occur on the disc. If a song is a cover-tune, I would strongly recommend putting in at least the original artist, and even the name of the songwriter. Putting the soloist's name for each song is great too. If you have different people doing vocal percussion from song to song, this is a good place to list their names as well.

Production Credits

I like to look at albums that I dig, and see how they've done this. Grab your favorite U2, Guster, Moby, or whatever, and see how the credits are worded. It's definitely a good starting point. Here's an example of how I did the credits on the *Dark Side of the Moon A Cappella* CD:

Recorded and Mixed by: Freddie Feldman at VOCOMOTION, Evanston, IL
Mastered by: Doug Sax at The Mastering Lab, Ojai, CA
Produced by: Freddie Feldman
Arrangements by: Jon Krivitzky
Music Director: Jon Krivitzky

Thank You Lists

Some groups put "Special Thanks" and "xxxx Would Like To Thank" in their liner notes; some don't. I always like to do it. People really dig seeing their name in print, and if they helped put your album together in any way, it's a nice thing to do for them. It's up to you whether you do one long list of people or a separate list for each member of the group. The order of the names may mean something to you; it may not. Maybe the first and last names are the most important and the rest are alphabetical . . . it's up to you.

Keeping It Legal

To make an album containing non-original songs, you must pay a license fee to the Harry Fox Agency. Mechanical licensing is the licensing of copyrighted musical compositions for use on CDs, records, tapes, and certain digital configurations. The Harry Fox Agency was established as an agency to license, collect, and distribute royalties on behalf of musical copyright owners.

Under the United States of America Copyright Act, the right to use copyrighted, non-dramatic musical works in the making of phonorecords for distribution to the public for private use is the exclusive right of the copyright owner. However, the Act provides that once a copyright owner has recorded and distributed such a work to the U.S. public or permitted another to do so, a compulsory mechanical license is available to anyone else who wants to record and distribute the work in the U.S. upon the payment of license fees at the statutory "compulsory" rate as set forth in Section 115 of the Act.

It should be noted that a mechanical license does not include the right to reproduce an already existing sound recording. That is a separate right, which must be procured from the copyright owner of said sound recording.

The Harry Fox Agency issues mechanical licenses that are valid for products manufactured and distributed in the U.S. only (including its territories and possessions). Mechanical licenses are available only to U.S. manufacturers or importers with U.S. addresses.

A mechanical license does not include lyric reprinting or sheet music print rights. For these rights, you must contact the publisher(s) directly.

If you would like to obtain a license to make and distribute 2500 or less recordings within the U.S., you can get a Harry Fox Agency mechanical license at www.SongFile.com.

Do I Really Need to Do this Licensing Stuff?

Yes, you do. I know in the past, many scholastic a cappella groups have been hesitant to pay for licensing, but in the case of digital distribution, be careful. It would be easy for the RIAA to pull up a list of cover songs that are digitally distributed and then crosscheck that list with the license database at HFA. I'm not saying that it's a trivial task, but it's possible. It's also possible that in the near future, all of these systems will be linked together, to prevent artists from skirting around the licensing issue.

So, don't mess with it. Pay your fees and you'll be a happier person (the universe will thank you). Remember that you're also making money from songs that someone else took the time to write. Pay them for the masterpiece you've decided to honor by covering on your album. Pay the license fees.

Financing Your Project

All this stuff costs money, right? I've got a few suggestions that will help you raise money for your recording project. There are tons of ways to raise money—just get creative. Obviously, doing gigs for money is a great way to finance your project. Here are some others . . .

Pre-Sales

Many groups have successfully raised recording funds by pre-selling copies of their CD before it was even made. Come up with some ways to convince people to buy the CD. If you've got previous albums already made, play them clips to show them the quality of your recordings. Maybe mix a couple tracks from this new CD early so that you can have a "demo" of the new album. Get creative.

Alumni

This one really only applies to high school and college groups. Chances are, if you're reading this, your group is fairly new and you might not have a lot of alums just yet. But if your group has been around for several years, you may have alums that would be willing to kick in some money here and there. Make it worth their while; give them a couple copies of the CD for their donation. It winds up only costing you a few bucks. Maybe bring all the alums who have donated together for a special CD Release party. Make the alums feels special and they'll be more willing to help you with your CD.

Sell Ad Space in Your CD Booklet

I haven't had a lot of groups take me up on this suggestion, but it might work for you. Basically, approach local businesses and see if they'd be willing to pay to have their logo or small ad placed inside your CD booklet. This really doesn't cost you anything, but the businesses might get some great exposure from being there.

CHAPTER 25

The Sing-Off:
Lessons Learned

One of the most transformative events in the history of our a cappella program was when Eleventh Hour (EH) was selected as the first high school group to compete on NBC's *The Sing-Off*. This is not because of the standard notions about TV exposure, but because the audition process fundamentally changed our culture for the better.

Learning from Failure

I first heard of *The Sing-Off* (hereafter listed as *TSO*) when I received an email from a casting agent. Someone involved in the show was doing research on possible groups and saw some YouTube videos of Eleventh Hour. While we were interested in the possibilities of the show, we pointed out that our group was comprised of high school students, and as such didn't meet the age requirement of 18. We were told to come to the audition anyway, and that if we were selected, they would get parental consent to deal with the age issue.

Because my daughter was only a few months old, I wasn't in a position to make the drive to Chicago for auditions. EH wanted to give it a shot, and so they made the trek with a parent chaperone.

When they returned the next day, I got a complete rundown of the audition. The kids sang well, but they had only been together about three weeks (it was the start of the school year) and they were stiff. They got overwhelmed and froze up in front of the producers. One of the casting agents started shouting, "Move around! Move around!" and jumped up and down among the singers for encouragement. EH made it through one-and-a-half of their three song audition and came back home.

The students and parents all said the same thing: "They wanted us to do well. We could see that they were hoping we'd do well, but we just didn't. We froze." I asked EH what they would do differently if they had the chance to do it all over again. The answer: "We'd bring it. No more holding back."

TSO aired over the holiday break and we all watched the eight groups who were selected for Season 1. We enjoyed the show, but couldn't shake the ghost of that failed audition. I decided to turn the energy around. During rehearsals when energy was low or when individual preparation waned, I simply said, "Do it like you wish you had done it in Chicago."

> **Lesson learned:**
>
> Sometimes you only get one shot to do something right. Give it your all, and if someone asks you to change for the better, do it. Don't let fear stop you from growing, or you'll live to regret it.

A Shot at Redemption

In the spring, *TSO* was renewed for a second season. Wonder of wonders, we got another casting email. I called EH into my office and asked them, "Do you want another shot at *The Sing-Off*?" They all said yes. After reading the casting announcement, I said, "If we do this, we can't play around. We aren't just prepping to get on the show; we're prepping to win."

The BHAG

What is a BHAG? Big Hairy Audacious Goal. Jim Collins and Jerry Porras coined it in their 1994 book, *Built to Last: Successful Habits of Visionary Companies*. They define a BHAG this way: "A true BHAG is clear and compelling, serves as unifying focal point of effort, and acts as a clear catalyst for team spirit. It has a clear finish line, so the organization can know when it has achieved the goal; people like to shoot for finish lines."

When we first auditioned for *TSO*, it was a lark. It didn't seem reasonable to think they would really want us on the show, so we didn't prepare adequately. The students just thought it would be a "neat experience."

Round two—well, that was a different story. Based on the overall interaction at Season 1 auditions, EH knew that they really had a shot at national television if they just dotted every "i" and crossed every "t." Getting on national television—that's a BHAG!

> **Lesson learned:**
>
> A BHAG is a galvanizing experience that is more motivating than "regular" rehearsals and concerts.

Training

In order to prepare for Season 2 auditions, we used the second habit from Steven Covey's *7 Habits of Highly Effective People*: begin with the end in mind. In order to prepare for success, we had to document what happened at the first audition, then break it into pieces, practice each piece, then reassemble them. We determined that our first audition came down to four components: singing, interview skills, group identity, and overall comportment. Then we had to consider all the general details, including such minutia as the size of each room and with whom we would interact.

The singing part was the easiest to handle. Naturally, we work on singing all year long. The biggest hurdle was to ensure we had energy to spare while performing and that we were never perceived as stiff. For the singing portion, we estimated the size of the performance space, and then recreated it in a special way. We put show choir platform risers together to make a mini-stage. That way, the singers knew exactly how much space they had to cover. We then created a visual plan for each song, changing positions regularly and creating opportunities to do coordinated, big moves. It wasn't a choreography plan; it was a visual energy plan.

The next part of the process was interviewing. We started by making a list of every question we could remember from the Season 1 interview. In addition, we added questions that *might* be asked. Each singer was given the list and an assignment to write out their answers. We read the answers aloud and decided which were the best. Everyone got a study sheet of the questions and the new "best" answers. We brought in a public relations specialist (my wife) to teach the singers interview techniques and run practice sessions. We found a room in the music wing that was roughly the same size as the audition site's interview room and practiced over and over.

From our Season 1 audition and from watching the show, we could tell that having a group identity was going to be important. Being high school students, we didn't have much life experience on which to draw. However, we did notice that each singer had a unique personality. Eleventh Hour did encompass many types of students. We decided to fill out our audition packets in a way that would highlight the students' personalities. Among the group, we had:

» The homecoming queen

» An Irish dancer

» An artist

» A computer "geek"

» A former athlete

» An honor student

» A songwriter

This led the producers to portray us as the "Breakfast Club," a group where many different types of students came together through their love of a cappella.

The last part of our preparation was on general comportment. We practiced how to enter rooms. We practiced what we would do when we were told to wait. We practiced how to speak to the producers in a casual setting (not the interview). At all times, we resolved to be upbeat, positive, engaging, and always smiling.

Lessons learned:
- Begin with the end in mind.
- There's more to your group than singing.
- Everything takes more preparation than you think in order to be outstanding.
- When working toward a goal, replicate the situation as much as you can— if competing on a large stage, practice on a large stage (and so on).
- Control everything you can control.

The Audition

We had done all we could to prepare for our audition, so we were excited when we arrived in Chicago. Unfortunately, there were more groups present than anticipated, and so our assigned "preferred audition time" was pushed back later and later. After hours of waiting, the kids were starting to lose energy. Finally, it was our turn.

I pulled EH together and said: "I am incredibly proud of you all. You've done an enormous amount of work this year and have really outdone yourself getting ready for this audition. I don't know if you're going to get on the show, but you have the ability to show the producers the group you really are. Just remember this—you will never get this chance again. Whatever you do in this room will be it, period. If you do all you can and don't get on this show, you can still be proud of yourselves. If you don't do all you can during this audition, that's fine, too, but I never want to hear about it. We will never again say 'coulda-woulda-shoulda.'"

The audition went great. The kids blew the producers away. From the back of the room, I could see EH lighting up the stage and the producers conversing with their heads nodding. When it was over, we were enthusiastically thanked, then led back to the holding tank to await our interview.

While waiting for the interview, we were approached by a producer who said, "Do NOT leave this building without seeing me." We took that as a good sign.

Another good sign came at the start of the interview. There was one lone woman in the room with her video camera. I was told that I would not be allowed to speak (*The Sing-Off* doesn't allow directors to assist groups in any way). The woman looked at our audition packet and said, "Wow . . . it says here 'These guys are sooooooooo good! Seriously. So good.'" (She even counted the "o"s for emphasis.) After she asked many questions, she began talking to herself in a low voice: "If I put you in front of five million people, are you gonna clam up on me? Are you gonna clam up? What are you gonna do?" I couldn't take it any longer. I said, "I'm sorry. I know I'm not supposed to talk, but these kids are clutch players. They will deliver, I guarantee it." She changed her posture and said, "Okay, I have some more questions."

After the interview, we were escorted outside to make a test video for the producers at NBC. That meant we were on the "short list" but not yet on the show. Little did I know as we drove back home from Chicago (arriving in Kettering at 3:00 a.m. with 8:00 a.m. exams for the kids the next day) that our audition had only just begun.

Lessons learned:

- Preparation pays off.

- If you prepare adequately and perform to the best of your ability, you can be proud of yourselves and avoid regrets. You can't control what others do, but you can control yourselves in order to maximize your chances of success in any situation.

The Post-Audition Audition

While we were now on the "short list," we had a period of about three weeks during which we continued to have some form of prolonged audition. Producers called various members of the group independently to ask them questions about their home lives, their school habits, and many other things to get a sense of whether our "home story" would be interesting to the viewers. We also had many discussions of the logistics that occur when minors appear on TV, legal issues that involved the school district and much more. Thankfully, we won out and were chosen to be one of ten groups on Season 2. The fun was just beginning.

Making the Show—The Prep Work, Performance, and Post Game

Prep Work

After being informed in late June that we were selected for the show, we were slated for a mid-July "home story" filming. We also had mountains of paperwork to complete, and the producers were constantly asking us for "demo" versions of songs to see if they were a good fit for the show. I would get a call on Monday asking for a demo of a song to be ready by Wednesday. This happened on many occasions. We decided to alleviate the problem of scheduling by agreeing to meet for rehearsal every day at 3:00. If there was nothing new to do, we'd split. If we had a demo to learn and record, we'd do that. We also had a song to learn for the home story ("Don't You Forget About Me" from the movie *The Breakfast Club*). During this period we learned the value of communication, the benefit of constant contact, and the challenge of learning a lot of new music quickly. Some of those benefits show up in other chapters in this handbook.

Lesson learned:

Do whatever the situation demands. The bigger the success, the bigger the investment.

Performance

In August we hopped a plane and headed for Los Angeles. Eleventh Hour left first, then I followed three days later. I knew in advance that I wouldn't be allowed to direct in any way, but I wanted to be around as a source of support. EH had to do everything themselves, just like the "big boys." They had costume fittings, rehearsals for the mass opening numbers, individual coachings, and many (many, many) adjustments to the arrangements they were to sing on the show. At one point, a staff arranger worked through the night to create the arrangement of "Just the Way You Are," which EH performed on the second episode. In order to make sure we didn't lose a minute of rehearsal, the arranger drove to a fast-food restaurant on a corner we would pass on our way from the hotel to the studio. When the traffic light turned red, he came running into the street to throw seven copies of the music through our van window. The light turned green, and we were off again with the new song in hand.

Throughout all of this, I learned the immense positive impact of student ownership. The group grew immensely due to the time they spent in charge of their own destiny. Of course, every group still needs a director, but I challenge you to create ways that your group can own pieces of their own development. These concepts also appear throughout this book. The success of Eleventh Hour as a self-contained group in this environment was the ultimate "final exam." Everything they had ever learned was put to the test for three weeks in California, across sixteen-hour days with almost zero down time.

> **Lessons learned:**
> - High school students are more capable than you ever dreamed, given the chance to prove it.
> - Independence breeds growth, if monitored properly.

Post Game

Eleventh Hour was eliminated from *The Sing-Off* in the second episode. We returned home happy with our performance, and innocently thought that we would return to our everyday routine while we waited for the show to air in December. We couldn't have been more wrong.

The first thing that happened was the public announcement of the groups who made the show. We had newspapers and TV stations calling us for interviews and public interest segments. Our singers were regularly in front of the local media, so they had represent themselves well. We had to constantly remind ourselves of what we could say and could not say, and also communicate to the media what was "fair game." Certain aspects of the show were to be kept confidential. This process strengthened our internal communication and also taught the students the importance of *messaging*, the art of creating, and stating central themes that become "the party line."

The next curve ball came when we were asked to contribute a track to *The Sing-Off* Christmas album, *Harmonies for the Holidays*. Our lead singer, Kendall, had already moved to Nashville to attend Belmont University, so we had to coordinate her return to get "Santa Claus Is Comin' to Town" in the can. It was an invaluable experience for the students to play "studio singer," learning the music on their own for a one-day recording session.

The show aired, and we were eliminated. We watched the rest of the season play itself out. As the end drew near, we received the phone call that we were being asked back to L.A. for the live finale. It was quite a fun and unexpected experience, but the ride didn't end there. Sony had approved a *Best of Season 2* CD, and we had to do a hurry-up session (again) to record a studio version of Justin Bieber's "Baby." This time it was Christmas break and the snow was falling. Kendall made it back from Nashville, but just barely. We had to record quickly to avoid being snow-bound in a studio.

Lesson learned:

If you commit to a large project, be ready for unforeseen side projects.

The Positive Side Effects of *The Sing-Off*

The Growth of the BHAG

We mentioned the Big Hairy Audacious Goal. *The Sing-Off* certainly was one. After such a process, we saw with great clarity the value of dreaming big and haven't stopped.

Instant Credibility

National TV is something that nearly every person on the planet perceives as special. After being part of *The Sing-Off*, everyone began to see us differently. We were always well received, but now we were sought-after. Our choir department, which was always respected, took a huge leap upwards in the eyes of the community and within the school district. When we performed at the state music conference and at the American Choral Directors Association National Convention, the rooms were packed.

Gigs, CDs, and $

Immediately after being on television, we were inundated with phone calls for performance opportunities that had previously been closed to us. Many were entertainment spots on national conventions, but some others included performances in other states for youth programs and the like. Everywhere we went we sold many more CDs, and our gig fee went up dramatically. We even sold more digital downloads on iTunes. In a year that was financially tough for our booster program, Eleventh Hour's new caché was keeping our heads above water.

Opening Doors

The biggest benefit of being on the show was how it opened doors for us—as a group and for individuals. Our singers made industry contacts that will pay off as they start their careers. Some were even offered jobs or internships when they finished high school. We were contacted by *America's Got Talent* (we didn't go) and *Extreme Makeover Home Edition* (we did go, portraying Christmas carolers on their holiday special). Kendall was selected to return in Season 3. All in all, this was a great experience for the students, many of whom plan to make music their livelihood.

The Negative Side Effects of *The Sing-Off*

Living in the Shadow (Or Is it the Shade?)

Unfortunately, one of the downsides to a large accomplishment is that the group immediately following can sometimes feel as if they are living in the shadow of their predecessors. Between the summer taping, the interviews, both CD projects, and the live finale, Eleventh Hour was living a split life. The "Sing-Off" Eleventh Hour was still reconvening and doing things while the "next generation" Eleventh Hour was trying to find their own identity. While the three new members were very gracious, it had to get old for them. Every time we sang a gig, well-intentioned people would ask, "What was it like to be on TV?" Sometimes it was like having a raspberry seed in your teeth that you just couldn't get out. Still, we reminded ourselves that whatever is good for any Eleventh Hour is good for all Eleventh Hours. After all, the "next-generation" singers are the ones who got to go sing many more gigs as a result of the notoriety. So, rather than "living in the shadow" of the "Sing-Off" Eleventh Hour, we liked to think of it as staying in the shade. Thanks to their accomplishment, our lives were just a bit better moving forward.

Oversaturation

Another consequence of garnering so much attention is oversaturation. Although everyone in the choir department was happy for Eleventh Hour, there comes a time when enough is enough. After a few months, we could almost hear the other students thinking, "If I hear about Eleventh Hour one more time, I'm gonna scream!" It is a natural tendency of young people to think that the elevation of one group's value leads to the devaluation of all others. While that simply isn't true, it is a feeling that crops up. When your group does something extremely special, be prepared for such reactions and be sensitive. Always be proactive in letting your department know that a win for one is a win for all.

Is it Over Yet?

This is like internal oversaturation. At some point, Eleventh Hour began to joke: "Is it over yet?" While being on TV is grand, at some point everyone wants to be valued for his or her next phase of development. Having so many "add-ons" after the show finished taping (roughly six more months of obligations) sometimes had a feeling of tying us to the past rather than the future.

Summary

Being selected for *The Sing-Off* was the ultimate learning experience. While there were a few negatives that could not be foreseen, the vast majority of the process was incredibly positive on multiple levels for all involved. While not every group will be able to have experiences that involve national television, every group can create BHAGs for themselves and create ways to foster the type of educational experiences that they bring.

One thing I cannot over-emphasize—in order to achieve maximum growth, it is important that your train your students to perform as if they are a professional group. If you try to be a good high school group, that's the best you'll ever be. You might also fall short of that goal, and end up being just another high school group. However, if you train to be a professional group and fall short, you can still far exceed the normal high school expectations. There are many professional singers, actors, and dancers who aren't yet 18-years old. Why not train your students to shoot for the stars?

Acknowledgments

I sincerely thank the many people who contributed not only to this book, but to my development in the art form of contemporary a cappella. I consider them all mentors, colleagues, and most importantly—friends.

» Nathan Altimari – for his wonderful arrangements and his contributions to **The Solo Vocalist**
 www.naltimar.com
 www.firedrillband.com

» Shane Coe – for his contribution to **Your Visual Plan**

» Trist Curless of m-pact – for his many hours of Skype discussions on a cappella in general, and his contributions to **What About the Bass?**, **Microphone Technique**, and **Live Sound for Pop A Cappella**
 www.m-pact.com

» Jeffrey Delman – for urging me on, for reading everything, and for offering unique perspective as my "go-to guy."

» Freddie Feldman of VOCOMOTION Studios – for his generous studio scholarships to Eleventh Hour and for his chapter **Making A Recording**
 www.vocomotion.com
 www.beatboxmics.com
 www.acabootcamp.com

» John Gentry of JAG Recording Studios – for always going the extra mile to support the development of live sound and recording education at Kettering Fairmont and for his chapter **Live Sound for Pop A Cappella**

 www.JAGRecordingStudios.com

» Christopher Given Harrison – for the wisdom shared in **Effects (FX) Pedals**
www.christophonemusic.com
www.sonosings.com

» Benjamin McClain of SONOS – for assistance with **Vocal Percussion** and **Microphone Technique**
www.sonosings.com

» Jake Moulton of Mo5aic – for **Vocal Percussion**
www.jakemoulton.com
www.mo5aic.com

» Alex Phan – for being an amazing teaching partner, a strong force in Kettering Fairmont a cappella, and for his contributions to **Pop A Cappella in the Classroom**

» Jim Probasco – for hiring me, encouraging me, and helping me navigate my initial contacts in the world of publishing

» Brad Rees of Tiffin University – for inspiring me to start down this path through his amazing group Up In the Air, and for constant guidance in the early days
www.tiffin.edu
www.upintheair.us

» **Deke Sharon** – for guiding me into the a cappella community, for countless arrangements, for helping me find resources when I was flying blind, for *The Sing-Off*, and for his foreword.

» **Michael Spresser** and Alfred Music Publishing Co., Inc. – thank you for taking a chance on contemporary a cappella

» The members of SONOS, Firedrill!, m-pact, and The Fault Line – for bringing magic to Kettering Fairmont High School and continually sharing of themselves selflessly for years afterward to help us grow.

The publisher wishes to thank the following for the use of the photographs throughout the book:

» Snake image (page 133) provided by C.B.I. Cables
» Cable and connector images (page 135) provided by Neutrik®
» A Cappella Records: The Duke's Men, Loreleis
» A Cappella Fest: Chapter 6
» Centerville High School: Forte
» Firedrill!
» Girls Next Door
» Jake Moulton
» Kettering Fairmont High School: Eleventh Hour, Fusion
» Transit
» Undivided